S.I.M.P.L.E. PREACHING

ROC COLLINS

innovo
PUBLISHING

Published by Innovo Publishing, LLC
www.innovopublishing.com
1-888-546-2111

Providing Full-Service Publishing Services for Christian Authors,
Artists & Ministries: Hardbacks, Paperbacks, eBooks, Audiobooks,
Music, Screenplays, & Courses

S.I.M.P.L.E. PREACHING

ISBN: 978-1-61314-614-9
Library of Congress Control Number: 2020950642

Cover Design & Interior Layout: Innovo Publishing, LLC

Printed in the United States of America
U.S. Printing History
First Edition: 2020

Dedicated to my wife
Jeralyn
and my sons
Ro and Noah.
They have made my journey sweet!

CONTENTS

FOREWORD

When I heard Roc Collins preach, my preaching was transformed, and it's never been the same since. Roc doesn't preach the same way I preach. I don't preach like he preaches. But my preaching has monumentally changed—and changed for the good—because of Roc's influence.

Roc and I were classmates in the doctoral program at New Orleans Baptist Seminary. Back then, he was serving as a full-time evangelist in Mississippi. I was pastoring a small church in rural southeast Louisiana. I invited Roc to come preach for our church's spring revival. That week, I listened to a preacher unlike any I had ever heard before. His messages were marked by . . .

The sweat of hard work and exertion blended with confident reliance on God's Spirit.

Delivery that was equally self-forgetful and transparent in revealing the preacher's unique personality.

Graciousness mixed with get-real boldness.

Passionate earnestness tempered by affability and good humor.

Expositional depth accompanied by evangelistic drive.

Preaching that's not afraid to get loud but also able to get out of the way and let the still, small voice of God speak.

The Spirit of the Lord moved in those services as Roc Collins preached, both in the congregation and in my own heart. I asked for God to help me—within the expression of my own calling, gifts, and temperament—to preach with the same freedom and passion I heard in my brother. I'll say it again: *my preaching has never been the same.*

Over the years since, I've heard my friend Roc preach in all kinds of settings, and I am always blessed and encouraged by his messages and by him personally. More than that, he and I have spent hours and hours learning from one another and sharpening each other's understanding of what it means to preach the Word of God.

Reading *S.I.M.P.L.E. Preaching* has had the same effect on me as hearing Roc preach for the first time or sitting with him over a cup of coffee, talking "preacher talk." This book inspires me to deeper love and passion for Jesus and compels me to dig into the Bible week by week, study to understand the passage's meaning, prepare a message that communicates clearly, and then preach with Spirit-filled abandon. And, because Roc has a pastor's heart, he knows the struggles pastors face and how to both boost our esteem and rebuke any hint of defeatism that might creep into our thinking.

I'm thankful for Dr. Roc Collins. And I'm grateful that he has written this profound book on *S.I.M.P.L.E. Preaching*.

—Stephen Rummage, Ph.D.
Senior Pastor, Quail Springs Baptist Church, Oklahoma City

INTRODUCTION

G od has always had a word.

John begins his poetic narrative with this simple declaration: "In the beginning was the word. And the Word was with God and the Word was God." With this Word, He whispered stars across the far reaches of the universe, and out of *nothing* spoke every *something* into existence.

And since the fall of man, God has always had a preacher. The first sermon was simple. It echoed through the garden in the form of a question: "Adam, where are you?"

Noah preached for decades with no converts, no revival, no believers. He preached and kept hammering away.

Abraham preached to his family. He called them to follow him on a one-way trip into unknown territory.

Joseph preached to his brothers on forgiveness.

Moses preached to Pharaoh and a fickle, foolish nation.

Joshua preached the Word of God to Israel to be strong and courageous against all odds.[1]

David preached to a towering bully hell-bent on blasphemy.

Solomon preached wisdom to a nation filled with folly.

Elijah preached to the prophets of Baal, a bunch of backslidden witch doctors with a prescription for damnation, and fire fell from the heavens.

Nehemiah preached to lazy fathers who fell asleep at the wheel, as their sons married Moabite women.

---

1. Joshua 10:25

Jeremiah preached in dry fields with no sign of harvest, no responses, no rewards.

Amos preached the Word of God, demanding justice for the poor, hope for the hungry.

When Ezekiel preached in a bone yard, tissue, sinew, muscles, and bones reshaped themselves into an army.

Isaiah, Joel, Micah, Zechariah, and every prophet, from the minor to the major, preached of the glorious One who is to come!

Jesus preached as the Word became flesh and dwelt among us. He preached good news. He was the message in flesh and blood. As He lived and died, He surely taught us to love one another.

And every preacher who followed Jesus aspired to make the name of Jesus known to the nations. A once stumbling, garish man called Peter made a rock-hard declaration on the day of Pentecost, and three thousand men were baptized, plunging themselves into the cleansing fountain of newfound grace. Stephen preached as the stones rained down on him. Paul preached on Mars Hill, giving the unknown God a name which is above every name.

Through the centuries, others followed. We remember some of their names: Martin Luther, John Knox, Phillip Brooks, Matthew Henry, Oswald Chambers, John Whitefield, John Wesley, Billy Sunday, A. W. Tozer, Adrian Rogers, and W.A. Criswell. All of them differ in style, era, and story, but are bound by the ultimate epic of the Gospel message.

There are others we'll never know this side of glory, who preached in the obscure outposts of the Kingdom. We'll never know all their names. How could we? Yet they were just as important to God as the names we studied in church history classes. These were the men who were faithful to the inerrant Word of God, who preached the Word, in season and out of season. They reproved, rebuked, and exhorted with all patience and teaching.[2]

And now here we are, preacher. Pick your walk-up music, because *you* are up to bat. This is our time! Eternity hangs in the balance. How faithful will we preach God's Word? Preaching God's Word is one of the most challenging vocations a man might undertake. But it's also simple, like doing push-ups. You can learn to do push-ups in a matter of minutes, but how many men do you know that can do two hundred? Hemingway once remarked that writing is *simple.* All you have to do is sit down and bleed. I think the same is true for preaching. It's not a difficult intellectual practice. I've seen a simple cornbread preacher shake the rafters of hell and the most learned scholar become the best antidote for insomnia.

In this book I will share six steps to practical preaching. These steps are S.I.M.P.L.E.:

1. **S**tart with Prayer,

2. **I**nvest in the text,

3. **M**aximize the message,

4. **P**reach,

5. **L**eave it all in the pulpit, and

6. **E**xtend and invitation.

This small book is not a theological dissertation on hermeneutics, soteriology, or polemics. It's a book *for* preachers, *of* preachers, and *by* a preacher. If you were to ask me what my primary passion and calling is for the time on this blue marble, it's to preach the Word. My prayer is that this book will fuel the fire burning within you to boldly proclaim that Jesus saves.

---

2. 1 Peter 4:2

1

START WITH PRAYER

"You will never be stronger in the pulpit than you are on your knees."
—Roy O. Collins, Jr.

I can't wait to meet George Mueller in the corridors of glory. Here's a singular man that opened 117 orphanages in England that provided a safe place for over ten thousand boys. Then he retired at age seventy. Time to kick back and enjoy your retirement, George! Right? Not exactly. In his retirement, he traveled over two hundred thousand miles preaching the Gospel. Also keep in mind that he did this before the advent of air travel. The most astounding Mueller quote I've read is this one:

> *The primary business I must attend to every day is to fellowship with the Lord. The first concern is not how much I might serve the Lord, but how my inner man might be nourished.*

This high-energy, active, serving, preaching legend said the most important ministry he had was not preaching. It was his prayer closet.

Powerful preaching *doesn't* come first. Preaching before prayer reminds me of the story of the old Cajun Boudreaux, who bought a brand-new chainsaw at the advice of a friend. He brought it back a week after using it. The chain looked dull, and splinters and pieces of bark were sticking out of it from all directions. The hot-tempered Boudreaux explained to the hardware store manager that he'd been using it all week and he was fed-up with the new-fangled tool. The store owner took it to the back, pulled the starter rope, and it came alive with a loud roar. Boudreaux, startled and perplexed, yelled back to the manager, "What's dat noise!"

I'm convinced that so many preachers are like that. They don't pull the starter rope of prayer, and their efforts are shrouded in futility.

DON'T BE A PRAYERLESS PREACHER

Prayer must be activated, or you'll grieve your church, your family, your staff, and most of all the Holy Spirit. When prayerless preachers stand behind the sacred desk, they are saying that famous line of all three-year-olds: "I'll do it myself." You might get away with it for a while, but it'll catch up with you in the long run. Satan has a heyday with prayerless preachers. He wrecks their homes, draws them into discouragement, leads them into temptation, and ultimately, he'll sabotage the calling on their lives.

Allow me to ask you a question. How does your prayer life compare to the other time priorities of your life such at TV, sports, fishing, golf, or other activities that fill your life? Our values on time are eschew these days. We think that someone who prays for an hour is a legendary spiritual warrior, but we *also* say that a guy who watches an hour of football is barely a fan. What's wrong with this picture? We ought to be "praying always with all prayer and supplication in the Spirit, being watchful to this end with all perseverance and supplication for all the saints!" (Ephesians 6:18).

I remember the truth W. A. Criswell spoke many years ago: "It's a strange thing in the life and ministry of our Savior; He never taught His disciples how to preach, but He taught them how to pray. It is far better that a minister of the Gospel knows how to pray well than it is even to preach well. If he's talking to God; then speaking to man will be easy."[3] Preacher, if your prayer closet is occupied only a few minutes a day, what in God's Kingdom are you doing? I think you'd have to agree . . . not much! If we're going to be honest, most preachers are preaching much longer every week than praying.

A few years back, a study by the Edison Research Group for LifeWay Christian Resources of the Southern Baptist Convention surveyed a nationally representative sample of 860 Protestant church pastors and found that most pastors pray an average of twelve minutes a day.[4] Is there any wonder why churches are closing their doors and baptisms are significantly dropping each year? If we are going to have the anointing of God, if we are going to see the fire of revival rekindled in our churches, if souls are going to be saved, if marriages are going to be restored, if the Gospel is going to transform our world, we must *start with prayer!*

> *If we are going to have the anointing of God, if we are going to see the fire of revival rekindled in our churches, if souls are going to be saved, if marriages are going to be restored, if the Gospel is going to transform our world, we must start with prayer!*

My prayer is that you won't skip over this chapter. I hope I've made a strong enough case that this is the real problem with preaching today. *This is important.* It's like using a chainsaw without pulling the starter rope. I hope you feel my index finger planted firmly into your chest as I ask you to

---

3. https://wacriswell.com/sermons/1988/lord-teach-us-to-pray/
4. http://www.bpnews.net/20918/most-pastors-unsatisfied-with-their-personal-prayer-lives

sincerely appraise your prayer life. As my high school coach would say, "Don't make me grab you by your face mask to get you to look me in the eyes to hear this."

Over the next few pages I'd like to share a pattern for prayer. It's an inventory that I've used for years, and if you really pray this way, you'll see your preaching bear fruit far beyond anything you've experienced in the prayerless preaching state.

1. PRAY FOR YOUR PERSONAL LIFE AND WALK WITH THE LORD

I'd call this part of prayer "illumination." It's asking God to reveal your true heart. This part requires silence and standing in the space of your prayer closet. You pray the prayer of David when he prayed:

Search me, O God, and know my heart;
Try me, and know my anxieties;
And see if there is any wicked way in me,
And lead me in the way everlasting.
(Psalm 139:23-24)

It takes some time for me to settle and listen, which is exactly what this part of prayer is all about. I am inviting the Holy Spirit to teach me what's broken inside my life. We don't burst into the throne room with requests or even worship. We're not ready for that at this point. We come in and stand in this holy space and allow the Lord to survey the landscape of our private world.

Lord, what is it that you want me to see about my soul? This is the question we must bring as we inquire of the Lord. It's not about the sermon series you are working on. It's not about the deacon that's been hounding you since the last finance committee meeting. It's not about the decision you are mulling about from the church pulpit committee that called you yesterday. *This time is about your heart.* Have a journal and a pen close by. Let God inventory your attitudes and motives—even more than your actions. This phase of prayer is not a time of talking to God but rather the Holy Spirit's quiet inventory of the condition of your heart. The Holy Spirit will begin to reveal the sin that has found comfortable living quarters in your heart. Seeking God is not knowing *about* God. It is knowing *Him.* It's personal, not merely theological. You have no right to preach on a passage without a willingness to completely submit to it.

Here's a list of gut-level questions that I believe God can use to help you as you go through this process of illumination:

- How much time have I spent over the past few days in prayer and Bible study for the sole purpose of fellowship with God?
- Is there anything that has seized the throne of my heart over the Lordship of Christ?
- How is my relationship with my wife and children?
- Have I spent quality time with my family?
- Have I engaged in any flirtatious attitudes or conversations that have compromised my sexual integrity?
- Am I guilty of not practicing what I am preaching?
- Do I have any impure motives or shadow-missions hiding in my heart?
- Am I getting enough rest? Have I kept a weekly sabbath?
- Have I met with my accountability partner this week?
- Have I taken care of my body over the past few days?

- Am I holding any bitterness or unforgiveness?

- Am I moving in the right direction toward spiritual closeness with Christ?

- Have I been generous—giving at least a tithe to my church and offerings to other ministries?

After you've spent time searching your heart using these and other questions, make the commitment to redirect your life. This leads to the second movement of prayer.

2. CONFESS THE SIN AND GET RID OF IT

It's about a word we don't hear in a lot of sermons these days: *Repent*. Nothing else really matters until you do. Nothing! Let's return to the voice of C. H. Spurgeon:

> You cannot preach conviction of sin unless you have suffered it. You cannot preach repentance unless you have practiced it. You cannot preach faith unless you have exercised it. True preaching is artesian; it wells up from the great depths of the soul. If Christ has not made a well within us, there will be no outflow from us.

There has never been a time that I have come into the prayer closet and have found myself clean from the start. My heart is always weighed and found wanting. But what a joy it is when I leave forgiven and rectified through the grace of Christ!

During this time of confession, the Holy Spirit may prompt you to make a call to reconcile with someone. There's a seldom used three-word sentence that carries tremendous weight in the realm of spiritual growth: *"I was wrong."* When we are willing to confess to others our mistakes and sins, we receive a more significant and powerful voice. But let's face it. We often refuse to admit our mistakes because of the illusion that preachers must always be seen as right. This is especially powerful in the family. Have you ever been in a disagreement with your wife and suddenly realize that you were on the wrong side of the argument, but you continue to try to make your point out of pride? When the realization happens, we have a moral and spiritual decision to make. We can win an argument, or we can be wrong and move to reconciliation. If we choose to win the argument, we lose so much more. Besides, let's get real. How many times has your marriage improved because you won an argument?

There's a seldom used three-word sentence that carries tremendous weight in the realm of spiritual growth: "I was wrong."

This is especially true when it comes to our children. If they don't witness our willingness to confess, they will reap the fruit of your pride and will never learn that skill as they grow up. Confession of your mistakes and sins allows them to see that you are real and growing as a believer. If you can't do this, you are giving them a clear picture of what a Pharisee looks like.

Every preacher needs to guard his heart when it comes to bitterness, pride, argumentativeness, and resentment. Let's keep in mind Paul's words:

> *Therefore, putting away lying, "Let each one of you speak truth with his neighbor," for we are members of one another. "Be angry, and do not sin": do not let the sun go down on your wrath, nor give place to the devil. (Ephesians 4: 25-27)*

If you want to preach hollow messages with little results, then marinate in your anger. Confession leads seamlessly into the third region of this prayer time.

3. GIVE GOD PRAISE, AND THANK HIM FOR HIS BLESSINGS

We know that God inhabits the praises of His people. Even more so does He empower the praises of His preachers. Just as Jehoshaphat appointed singers to march in front of the army (2 Chronicles 20), we must appoint our praises before our preaching.

Some might ask why I've put confession and repentance before worship. In my walk with the Lord, I have learned that I can't fully praise until I am pure before Him. My praise is the ultimate response to the work of forgiveness and cleansing He has wrought in my life. It's His greatest work. Remember Jesus' words: "For which is easier, to say, 'Your sins are forgiven you,' or to say, 'Arise and walk'?" (Matthew 9:5). We think about the wonder and majesty of God's work of Creation—the way He set the stars in place and caused the earth to tilt on its axis to birth the four seasons of the year. But His greatest work happens in our hearts. Often in Scripture, we see God referring to Creation as something done from the works of God's fingers, but when God refers to our forgiveness, reconciliation, and redemption, we read that this great reality is the work of His arms. He put galaxies in place with His fingers, but my salvation took upper body strength! Our forgiveness is the greatest miracle of all!

When we consider our right standing with God, there's nothing we can do but thank the Lord for His grace. G. K. Chesterton got it right when he said, "The worst moment for an atheist is when he is really thankful and has no one to thank." We have Someone to thank, and we should do it before we begin the process of proclaiming anything from His Word.

As John Oatman wrote in 1856:

So amid the conflict, whether great or small,
Do not be discouraged; God is over all.

Count your many blessings; angels will attend,
Help and comfort give you to your journey's end.[5]

I don't know about you, but I want the angels attending during this holy time of sermon preparation.

One of the greatest things about thanksgiving in prayer is that our gratitude will chase away the discouragement that often dogs us as preachers. Satan loves discouraging preachers. He so desperately longs to shut us up by giving us the Monday morning blues. When we aren't in the spirit of gratitude, we view yesterday with a blind eye to all that God did and hyper-focus on the one sarcastic comment from the old lady who sits on the back row scowling. We all know that lady, don't we? We've all heard that voice scoffing sarcastically, "I was here long before you got here, and I'll be here long after you leave." To that, we have to give a good southern, "Bless your heart," and get on with the great task God has called us to do.

Discouragement comes in many forms for all pastors— staff conflict, financial deficits, members heading out the doors of our church, moral failings of members, threats, prodigals, negative comments about toe-smashing messages, and a thousand other spiritual shocks that shrink our zeal. My first impulse is to complain to Jeralyn, my wife, about my frustrations. (Just a side-note: your wife is the weaker vessel, and she can't carry the burden of your frustration by herself. The first thing we need to do is tell it to Jesus.)

The last thing we need to do in times of adversity and spiritual warfare is to stop praising God. We get in trouble when we lose our song and give into the groaning. During advent of the exile, the psalmist wrote,

By the rivers of Babylon,
There we sat down, yea, we wept

---

5. "Count Your Blessings," a hymn. Public domain.

When we remembered Zion.
We hung our harps
Upon the willows in the midst of it.
(Psalm 137:1-2)

Don't make the mistake of living out a dry, voiceless, harp-hanging ministry. Paul and Silas would remind us that earthshaking things happen when we turn our groans into song.

I remember decades ago, I served in a church for a *decade* in *one year*. It was such a difficult year that I often went to bed wondering if I shouldn't just pack it in. One Sunday morning, I picked up a very pointed, anonymous one-sentence note that was left on my desk at the office. It simply said, "I'll kill you!" Like Elijah, I wanted to flee into the wilderness. But I survived because I knew God was at work, and He was and is bigger than the Judases and Jezebels of any congregation. It wasn't easy. I wouldn't want to go back to that place. But private worship and thanksgiving carried me through the nights my pillow was soaked in tears. I learned that once you praise Him in the midst of your crucible, God shows up and shows off. That's just how He works, and it all begins with praise. Joni Eareckson Tada reminds us, "Whatever troubles are weighing you down are not chains. They are featherweight when compared to the glory yet to come."[6]

Once you praise Him in the midst of your crucible, God shows up and shows off. That's just how He works, and it all begins with praise.

An old preacher once shared this strange story of a caged bird that got out of his cage when no one was looking. The bird flew out of the house in the middle of a blizzard and froze in mid-air. A few minutes later, someone opened

6. Joni Eareckson Tada, "366 Sparkling Devotions," from *Diamonds and Dust* (Grand Rapids, MI: Zondervan, 1993).

the door and threw some garbage on top of the bird. The bird miraculously began to get warm, defrost, and start chirping. A cat came by, heard the chirping, cleaned him up, and swallowed him whole. The morals of the story are ones every preacher needs to take to heart:

1. Sometimes your escape is worse than your present situation.

2. Not everyone who throws garbage on you is your enemy.

3. Not everyone that finds you and pulls you out of a mess is your friend.

And finally...

4. When you get garbage thrown on you, it's usually a good idea to keep your mouth shut.

I've often found that the best place to do your complaining is the prayer closet. But make sure after you finish, you begin to praise Him. Worship adjusts your attitude. It clarifies your purpose. It reminds you of His grace. It empowers your ministry. Only after you have confessed, worshipped, and given thanks are you ready to appeal to God for His guidance as you prepare to preach.

Here's a list of some of the things that preachers should ask God to do in the midst of our preparation:

Lord, I ask You to:

- Remove all distractions.
- Help me preach a message for Your glory and not mine.
- Guide me to the right resources.
- Help me to find Your voice.
- Overwhelm me with zeal for Your message.

- Grant me creativity and not imitation of other preachers.
- Bring the lost into a saving faith in You this Sunday.
- Convict me as I prepare, so that my words will be free from hypocrisy.
- Keep me from manipulating the Word for my own motives.
- Silence the voice of the enemy.
- Keep me from self-aggrandizement.
- Help me speak words that enter into the private lives of the people.
- Stoke my passion.
- Help me present the gospel.
- Help me as I make the appeal for everyone to take another step closer to You, especially me!
- TAKE OVER.

4. NOW LISTEN!

After you have gone through the process of listening, allowing the Holy Spirit to take an inventory of your personal, private world, confessing your sin and weakness before God, thanking and worshipping God, and asking Him to do the things listed here, *it's now time to return to listening.*

The word *meditation* carries some baggage because it's been hijacked by secularists and pagan mystics. But meditation is an important aspect of prayer. Early on in the pages of the Bible we find a challenge for God's people to meditate. God commands us to "Keep this Book of the Law always on your lips; meditate on it day and night, so that you may be careful to do everything written in it. Then you will be prosperous and successful" (Joshua 1:8 NIV). Notice that the focus of our meditation is Scripture. We don't stare mindless into the void of nothingness. We read the Word, and then in the silence of our prayer closet, we marinade our minds in Scripture. I'm not a speed-reader when it comes to reading the Bible. I'm amazed when some people say they read the Bible cover-to-cover in a month! I think that's amazing, but I hope they stop and meditate on every word and not just each chapter.

Whenever we read Scripture, God desires us to avoid racing through the Word. Rather, we should slow down and let the Scripture breathe. Over the years I've learned that if I'm doing it right, I'm not just working on Scripture, the Scripture is working on me. For the Scripture to truly work on me I need to give it time and my full attention.

Perhaps you've driven through a neighborhood in the community that had a reputation for Christmas lights. We had a neighborhood in our community that was so legendary that there would be bumper-to-bumper vehicles like the last scene in *Field of Dreams*. I'm sure you've slowed down to enjoy the lights in your town. So . . .

Let's not just read the Scripture. Let us revel in it!

Let's not just memorize Scripture. Let's let it mesmerize us!

Let's not just summarize chapters. Let's soak in the verses!

Let's not just underscore it with our pens. Let's underscore it on our hearts!

Let's not just hope in its promises. Let's plug into its power!

Whenever we slow down, listen, meditate, and pray, we are making our hearts fertile ground for proclamation. I must warn you though, meditating, being still, and resting in His presence takes practice. We live in a multi-tasking, noisy, online, never-say-stop culture. For me, it takes a couple of minutes to slow down the swirling thoughts and focus on God. But once you settle your mind, God's voice will come to you. But as you know, He speaks softly.

The Bible also mentions meditating on God's unfailing love (Psalm 48:9), on God's works and all His mighty deeds (Psalm 77:12), on God's precepts and His ways (Psalm 119:15), and on God's promises (Psalm 119:148).

Secular meditation leaves you without a resolution to your issues. You take a moment to clear the mind and then you're immediately back to your real, chaotic life. You may have a calmer disposition, but what you don't have is a solution to your real problems.

5. LISTEN AGAIN

Hopefully you've been listening intently through the whole time you've been fellowshipping with God. You must listen to Him until He has declared you forgiven. What a relief that we can come to Him just as we are, without one plea! Now is the time to settle ourselves once more to listen quietly as He speaks to us as pastors. We are listening to Him as we prepare to invest in the text. Before you open a commentary, write a word, open a software program or a browser, first listen.

6. BE THE RETRIEVER—WAIT FOR THE SIGNAL

I'm reminded of the correct posture by duck hunting with a Labrador Retriever. Just the experience of watching a well-trained dog speaks into the process of listening. On a cold morning, you go out to the lake and wait. Your eyes are scanning the horizon, waiting for that beautiful v-formation as the ducks fly across the horizon. You shoot, and one of the ducks falls from the flock with a splash, and the duck lands fifty yards in front of you. At that moment, the retriever's eyes turn to the hunter's. He's waiting for the signal. It doesn't matter how long he has to wait; he knows his job, and he's just going to sit and wait intently with focus on the word or the whistle his master gives. That intensity of waiting in the eyes, the ears twitching in anticipation for the word from his master, astounds me as a lover of dogs. Oh, that we would have that same intensity as we wait and listen for the word from the Master.

Waiting shouldn't be considered a passive act for the preacher. You've got to wait actively.

Waiting is not a passive act for the retriever. Waiting shouldn't be considered a passive act for the preacher. You've got to wait actively. G. Campbell Morgan says, "Waiting for God is not laziness. Waiting for God is not the abandonment of effort. Waiting for God means, first, activity under command; second, readiness for any new command that may come; third, the ability to do nothing until the command is given."[7]

Before we move on to the next chapter, I feel compelled to pray for you, my fellow preacher. This is my prayer for you!

God,

Help him to hear your voice louder than his most outspoken critic. Help him to laugh inside when people make veiled threats and impertinent demands upon him. Encourage him to be so bold in his message that people will want to cover their ears and chant "lalalala" to drown out

7. G. Campbell Morgan, *The Answer of Jesus to Job* (Eugene, OR: Wipf and Stock Publishers, 1935).

the ugly truth he proclaims. Give him a strong wife and intimacy. Being a preacher is not exactly the most romantic vocation, so he needs all the help he can get to keep the fire burning. May he have a strong stomach for the task. May he have at least three nights away from church activities. May he feel secure when shadow missions and finances make him feel like he is walking on a tight rope without a net. May he laugh between funerals and may his three suits and four ties look new when he wears them on those special occasions. May he not sound like any other preacher. Show him his voice and give him the grace to feel comfortable in it. May his fifteen-year-old car remind him of Abraham, the one who traveled by faith. Hold him together when the pieces fall apart. May he take his family to the beach even when a conference is not held there. Heal the loneliness that every pastor feels from time to time. Remind him that few understood Jesus, so he shouldn't assume that everyone will understand him either. I pray that he will not obsess about compliments, numbers, gossip, or the pastor down the street whose church is booming. May his baptistry waders not leak, and may his wireless microphone be free from ambient noise. May there be more movements in the hearts of people than there are in the nursery. May his Bible look like it's been through a hurricane because that's the forecast of our spiritual state in the world. Lord Jesus, preach to this preacher like he has never preached before.

In Jesus' name, amen!

SUMMARY: START WITH PRAYER

- Don't be a prayerless preacher.
- Pray for your personal walk with the Lord.
- Give God praise and thank Him for your blessings.
- Listen to God, and listen again.
- Receive what God says to you.

JOURNAL THIS

1. What are your greatest hinderances to prayer?

2. During what time and in what place do you set aside time to pray specifically about your preaching?

3. Who do you know is praying for you?

2

INVEST IN THE TEXT

"The Bible was not given for our information but for our transformation."
—*D. L. Woody*

I remember those long, hot, August two-a-days on the practice field as our position coaches would lead us through the drills in our playbook, over and over again. I thought some practices would never end. Conditioning, memorization, strategy, strength training, preparation, preparation, preparation! It's like that old analogy about the difference between contribution and investment. When it comes to the bacon and eggs that you eat at the breakfast table, the hen contributes but the pig is invested. For us, being invested in the text means more than contributing our opinions. The preacher has to be totally invested in the process. It takes time, tenacity, and fortitude to invest in the text. When it comes to preaching, the world doesn't need any more Saturday night specials.

For us, being invested in the text means more than contributing our opinions.

Remember how Paul coached Timothy: "Study to show thyself approved unto God, a workman that needeth not to be ashamed, rightly dividing the Word of truth" (2 Timothy

2:15 KJV). This verse reminds us that studying is important. Be the workman! Study! Why? So you can preach the Word.

Later in 2 Timothy we are challenged to "Preach the word! Be ready in season and out of season. Convince, rebuke, exhort, with all longsuffering and teaching" (2 Timothy 4:2). Over the years of preaching I've logged, this verse has been my touchstone—a life verse that reminds me of the reason God placed me on the earth for such a time as this. When we study the Word of God with an eye toward the pulpit, we are obeying the challenge of our brother Paul.

For the preacher, Sunday is the destination, but on Monday we suit up and begin to map out the plan for the next message we've been given to proclaim. I don't know about you, but for most pastors, Sunday rolls around once a week with extreme consistency! You have to turn off the noise and get busy. Whether you are preaching to ten or ten thousand, we have the great and high honor of lifting up the Word of God and bringing hope and transformation to people. In the smash and grab world we live in, we might succumb to the trap of forgetting both the awe and the wonder preaching brings.

Preaching remains indispensable. Remember the words of Paul:

> *How then shall they call on Him in whom they have not believed? And how shall they believe in Him of whom they have not heard? And how shall they hear without a preacher? And how shall they preach unless they are sent? As it is written: "How beautiful are the feet of those who preach the gospel of peace, Who bring glad tidings of good things!" But they have not all obeyed the gospel. For Isaiah says, "Lord, who has believed our report?" So then faith comes by hearing, and hearing by the word of God. (Romans 10:14-17 KJV)*

Notice the progression at the very end of the passage. Faith comes by hearing. Notice, faith's primary entry point is through the ears—not through the eyes, the touch, or experience. The world needs to hear the Word just as Paul heard the Word on the Damascus highway under flashing lights, or vertically challenged Zacchaeus heard from the branches of the sycamore, or as grief-stricken and available Isaiah heard under the shaking doorposts of the temple. People need to hear. But the question remains, *How will they hear without a preacher?*

Do you remember the first time you stood in front of a crowd to preach? I sure do. I'd seen my dad preach for years, but seeing preaching and actually doing it are two different things. In 1984, I preached my first sermon—and I still get butterflies in my stomach just thinking about it. I was as nervous as a cat on a hot tin roof! At Central Baptist Church in Lenoir, North Carolina, I walked up to the pulpit with knees knocking, a few scribbled notes, and the text of Mark 1, and I preached on the baptism of Jesus. I have a better grasp on the process and more experience under my belt after thirty-plus years of preaching, but I still have nervous zeal for the Word of God. I hope every preacher does, because if you don't, you're doing it wrong. This is holy work! How could a preacher make the Word of God boring with such a swashbuckling, miraculous, transforming Book from the Creator of the universe. In fact, if somebody ever told me the Bible was boring, I'd have to wonder if we were reading the same book! It contains . . .

- Lion hunts
- Giant death matches
- Angel wrestling
- Jail songs
- Honeymoon bride mix-ups

- Blazing chariots
- Talking mules
- Blood moons
- Sword fights
- Fire-walking
- Streakers
- Supernatural apparitions
- Shipwrecks
- Exorcisms
- Romance
- Nights afloat
- Blues songs
- Bear attacks
- Ambushes
- Snake pits
- Man-eating fish

This Book cannot be tamed. It's not a comedy of manners complete with tea and crumpets. It's gritty. It is real. It is perfect. It is divine. It is holy. Along with that, the Bible is an infinitely deep well of the riches of God. Adrian Rogers said it like this: "I have studied this Book, and I would never even dream of saying I've come to the bottom of the Word of God."[8]

It's gritty. It is real. It is perfect. It is divine. It is holy. Along with that, the Bible is an infinitely deep well of the riches of God.

The Bible has been described as a sword and a scalpel. It's powerful in the spiritual battle against unseen forces. And

8. Adrian Rogers, *What Every Christian Ought to know* (Nashville, TN: B&H Publisher, 2012) p. 25.

it is sharp enough to perform heart surgery and bring the sickest into wholeness. It is a microscope and a telescope. It can bring understanding to the infinitesimal mysteries of life while also revealing the mysteries of the universe. But most importantly, it reveals the mystery of salvation to all people!

No one can deny that the Holy Bible is the inseparable, seminal tool for effective preaching. Preaching without Scripture is like playing football without a ball. It's impossible. On top of that, it just doesn't make any sense. There's no sense in trying to say anything in your church if it's not Scripturally robust. That's why you need to invest in the text.

GUMBO AND THE GOSPEL

After a number of years serving in the New Orleans region during my seminary, I grew to love gumbo. As tradition has it, gumbo started in the 1760s with African slaves who combined whatever they could afford into a roux-based soup that was poured over rice. It's the combination of all the ingredients that makes gumbo glorious. No one would ever dare go to a pot of gumbo to fish out the chicken or the sausage or the oysters. That would be illogical and rude, to be honest. What makes gumbo so delicious and amazing is that all the unique and tasteful ingredients combine into the dark brown base to create a rich dining experience for the palette. I get hungry just thinking about it!

So what does this have to do with the Bible? The Bible is gumbo for the soul. All the elements of poetry, story, wisdom, worship, prophecies, miracles, blessings, law, grace, and salvation are poured together, and when we allow this Book to simmer in our souls over years, experience, sorrows, and joys, we find that it is irresistible. It's all in there! I had gumbo a few weeks ago, but I don't think, *That gumbo was good last week. I'll never want gumbo again because that's enough.* If you love gumbo, you'll be back for more. That's the way it is for the Bible and the believer. You aren't satisfied with one serving. You'll want to go back to the table time and time again.

I go back to the Bible for illustrations, prooftexting, worship, history, inspiration, prayer, encouragement, vision, purpose, humor, consolation, inspiration, direction, conviction, restoration, invitation, mystery, evaluation, explanation, blessing, and hope. We can go to the Bible for anything we face.

Let's return to the writings of Paul as he encouraged us to let our minds be transformed by the word:

> *But you must continue in the things which you have learned and been assured of, knowing from whom you have learned them, and that from childhood you have known the Holy Scriptures, which are able to make you wise for salvation through faith which is in Christ Jesus.*
>
> *All Scripture is given by inspiration of God, and is profitable for doctrine, for reproof, for correction, for instruction in righteousness, that the man of God may be complete, thoroughly equipped for every good work. (2 Timothy 3:14-17)*

I hope you don't spend your time in Scripture like a man with a ladle trying to fish out only those things that help your thesis, but that you will allow the whole counsel of God to speak in the pulpit. It begins with investing in the text.

HANDLE WITH HOLY CARE

This is divine, holy work. Every preacher should prepare with that in mind. If you treat the Bible casually as a preacher, you could drift into laziness, confusion, or even worse, heresy. Does it happen? All you need to do is look at the false doctrines that are being sold like lemonade in July online, in blogs, on Facebook, or on TV. It's everywhere, and it's the end result of "preachers" that have substituted style, glitz, and allure for solid biblical preaching.

If you treat the Bible casually as a preacher, you could drift into laziness, confusion, or even worse, heresy.

The Scriptural text must be the thrust of the message, not your own thoughts and opinions. I've known many preachers who begin with an idea and then comb the concordance to find Scripture that will support their premise. Let me assure you, that's not preaching. Preaching springs from the Word of God, which stands peerless above any truth, opinion, or idea. Before illustration, quotation, story, poem, statistic, admonition, or anecdote, Scripture demands to be the preeminent centerpiece of the message. Starting anywhere else is not only unwarranted, it can be dangerous.

Let's admit it, we sometimes hear a story and our first thought is, *That'll preach!* But really, no. Unless it begins with Scripture, nothing will preach. The Word comes first. The Bible has remained unimpeded through the centuries. It's been banned, burned, ridiculed, and hidden, but never defeated. Spurgeon said, "The Word of God is like a lion. You don't have to defend a lion. All you have to do is let the lion loose, and the lion will defend itself."[9]

It's important to have a systematic method of sermon prep. After years of mentorship, intense conversation with some of the greatest preachers alive today, and lots of trial and error, I'd like to share with you the process I use when preparing my messages.

---

9. Charles Spurgeon, in Glen G. Sorgie, Mark L. Strauss, and Stephven M. Voth, *The Challenge of Bible Translation* (Grand Rapids, MI: Zondervan, 2003).

Phase 1: Read the Text Thoroughly—Then Read It Again . . . and Again

We all know the shampoo instruction: Wash, rinse, repeat. That's a simple three-word plan. The pastor's preliminary instructions are that simple: you begin, pray, read, repeat. Our prayer should be to allow the Master Teacher, the Holy Spirit to teach us Scripture. If you invite Him into the process at the very beginning, this process of slowly reading Scripture will be time well spent. Otherwise, it's an exercise in futility. As you read, make sure you have a pen and paper close by. You'll always want to take notes when the Holy Spirit is teaching! As you begin reading and sermon prepping, don't make these common mistakes:

Discover What's Really Going On in the Text

Your preparation should be a dialogue with the Almighty as you study the text. If you prayerfully ask Him for inspiration, I know He will guide you. He'll show you new dimensions. Sermon preparation requires an initial openness to where the Lord leads you as you read and meditate on the text. It's not a one-session or even one-day process of study.

I'm sure you share a common experience with me. I wade into the text, and at first, the thoughts and truths are scattered like a jigsaw puzzle with little organization. It's like a whiteboard with various truths, ideas, and questions. Often I'll wake up in the morning and all the pieces seem to come together. So set it down, give your labor some space, and let God speak to you overnight.

Remember, Scripture First and then Application

Some pastors make the mistake of starting with topics and then cherry-picking Scriptures and using them as the proof text for the sermon. This works well in conversational evangelism, but for week-to-week sermon preparation, I've found it to be a deficient habit. Over time you'll find that you are not preaching the whole counsel of God. Some parts of Scripture will be ignored because they don't serve the purpose of the topic.

You also risk falling into the habit of choosing Scriptures to support the message rather than letting the Word properly speak for itself. It's tempting to lift a verse from Scripture and assign a meaning that pivots away from its original intent. Perhaps you've heard the old Bible professor's illustration: "You can't just pull out the verse, 'Judas went out and hanged himself,' and leapfrog to, 'Go thou and do likewise.'" Although this is an exaggerated illustration, we know that there are many pastors who take more subtle leaps frequently.

Here are two more common examples. Although the intent is pure, it's important to note the flaw in how these verses are utilized.

A Prophecy

> *Look among the nations and watch—Be utterly astounded!*
> *For I will work a work in your days Which you would*
> *not believe, though it were told you. (Habakkuk 1:5)*

Now if that's not a verse destined for the wall art section of a Hobby Lobby, I don't know what is. It could be cross-stitched on a pillow in the church parlor. It's inspiring and hopeful. Right?

But, let's look at the context. It's not hard. Just read a couple of verses after that, where we learn about God's ultimate threat of destruction of the people to whom this promise is speaking. God is sending the dreaded Chaldeans to wreak havoc on the people of God. So although Habakkuk 1:5 sounds like a great life verse, in its context it's not *exactly* the kind of amazement you'd ever really want.

A Promise

> *And I, if I am lifted up from the earth, will draw all peoples to Myself. (John 12:32)*

A preacher might pull this verse into a message about worship. It might sound something like this. "If we lift up and glorify Jesus, He will draw all people to Himself." But look at the context of the verse:

> *Jesus answered and said, "This voice did not come because of Me, but for your sake. Now is the judgment of this world; now the ruler of this world will be cast out. And I, if I am lifted up from the earth, will draw all peoples to Myself." This He said, signifying by what death He would die. (John 12:30-33)*

After you read the surrounding verses you understand the exact meaning of Christ's message through John's explanation. In verse 33, John clearly states that Jesus said this to describe how He would die. If you stop at verse 32, you'd missed the point, and you might end up taking a leap onto a faulty premise.

Pay Attention to the Voice of the Writer

It's imperative for the preacher to keep in mind who is speaking—and the circumstance. If you're knee-deep into church culture, you have heard it in songs, cheers, sermons, and pregame interviews of famous Christian athletes.

> *I can do all things through Christ who strengthens me. (Philippians 4:13)*

It's often referred to in contemporary circles like this: "I can solve this promise, score this touchdown, win that award, and (I'm sorry, but it's true . . .) marry that girl." This propagates a belief that supports a name-it/claim-it attitude regarding our ability to get what we want. But the person referring to the verse often forgets the voice of the writer.

Paul was in prison. In earthly terms, like with girls, football, acclaim, and financial success, Paul would seem like a loser. Paul is writing a letter *from prison* about being able to endure not achieve. He's enduring a loss of freedom, loneliness, uncertainty, and pain. Speaking in modern terms, this is not a prosperity kind of verse. It's an enduring kind of verse.

Now, you don't have to agree with me 100 percent, but I want to submit that Paul's voice, his circumstance, and the entirety of the book of Philippians is not well served by a trite, fist-bumping mindset that says, "I'm a winner!" Watch your toes. I'm dropping the mic.

> *In expository preaching, you aren't simply going on a fishing expedition to string together related verses on a subject. You are going through the narrative to understand what God is up to in the passage, while also realizing that you have to understand and ask some really important questions.*

Keep the Text In Context

This is the main reason expository preaching is so effective. In expository preaching, you aren't simply going on a fishing expedition to string together related verses on a subject. You are going through the narrative to understand what God is up to in the passage, while also realizing that you have to understand and ask some really important questions. In this initial study of the text, follow the five Ws of journalism: Who, What, When, Where, and Why.

Who Is Speaking?

What is the character, history, and experience of the writer, speaker, or character? We've got to remember that the Bible is a beautiful mosaic of history, wisdom, poetry, storytelling, prophecy, and drama. There is dialogue, narration, and characters speaking from their point of vision. Therefore, understanding who is speaking is important. That is what's so powerful about character studies in sermon preparation. If you understand Samson's upbringing, the tenants of the Nazirite vow, and his personality type, you are well on your way to exegeting his story and the meanings we encounter in the book of Judges.

What Is the Verse Saying?

What exactly does this message say? How does this passage fit into the overall chapter before the passage and after the passage? Sometimes we miss what's right under our noses if we don't look at what the verse actually says.

For example, take a look at Luke 15:10: "Likewise, I say to you, there is joy in the presence of the angels of God over one sinner who repents." I'm sure you've probably heard someone say or preach that when somebody gets saved, the angels rejoice. They use this as their prooftext, when in actuality, the verse doesn't say the *angels* rejoice. It says there is joy "in the presence of the angels." It's the saints that rejoice because only the saints truly understand what it's like to be lost and then experience salvation. It's just a few words, but if you're not paying close attention, you might miss an important and glorious detail.

When and Where Was This Written?

This is so important because every verse must be framed in the era it was written. God's precepts are timeless, but the time and era of the verse helps us and speaks into the way the message is presented and the timeless truths we capture from the verses. *History is important.* What was going on in the culture when the passage was written? *Progressive revelation is important.* It goes without saying that Peter, even though he was hard-headed, every now and then had more revelation than amazing Isaiah. He got to see more revelation by the simple fact that he was born later and happened to be a disciple of the Son of God Himself!

Why did God place the verses in the Bible? This question behooves us to zoom up and out to the thirty-thousand-foot view of the passage within the Scripture. We search the intent of God's story, precept by precept, verse by verse.

Follow Where the Teacher Leads

Don't go it alone. Bible study and Bible teaching will be cold, ineffective, and futile if you don't have Someone working with you. The Holy Spirit must guide you as you study Scripture or prepare to preach it. Scripture comes alive when we have a dialogue with the Source of all knowledge. This is what makes reading the Bible so incredibly transforming. There's something going on between the reader and the text. So prayer is a vital link to understanding the text.

So far we have surveyed just the first layer of preparation: read, pray through, and meditate on the text. This must happen first, but that, of course, isn't the end of the process. You've only laid the foundation and framed the house. Now you can lay the bricks.

Phase 2: Cross-Reference the Text

Martin Luther once said, "Scripture is its own expositor."[10] R. A. Torrey, in his study of the Bible, has over five hundred thousand cross-references.[11] With the foundation of the primary text in place, the second phase of my process is finding and correctly noting and utilizing

10. This axiom is universally sourced from Luther in Latin in the early 1500s. "Scripture sui ipsius interpres."

11. R. A. Torrey, *The Treasury of Scripture Knowledge: Five-Hundred Thousand Scripture References and Parallel Passages* (Peabody, MA: Hendrickson Publishers, 1988).

secondary texts that support the message of the primary text. You'll want to use the same litmus test for the secondary texts that you did with the primary text. Make sure you are taking note of the context of every Scripture you preach so you don't make the mistakes mentioned earlier.

There are a number of different ways you might choose to cross-refence a Scripture. Here's a list of some that you might want to utilize (and use a prompt or a punch list to help you through the cross-referencing process):

- Seek teaching verses that support the message of story Scriptures.

- Conversely, find story Scriptures that support teaching verses.

- Use poetry or imagery Scriptures to illustrate or emote the essence of complex themes.

- Use properly cross-referenced Scripture to create holy processes like prayer patterns, soul winning, or disciplining (e.g., the Romans Road).

- Cross-reference Scriptures relating to a biblical character's past actions or family history, which speaks into the motivations and proclivities of the figure.

- Use cross-referenced prophetic Scriptures to help explain events that happened in the Bible.

- Cross-reference verses that lay out a timeline of events that lead to the meaning of the primary text.

And speaking of cross-referencing Scripture in your sermon, I'd be at fault if I didn't offer some cautions.

Don't Lose the Focus of the Primary Text

Zoom out and look at the entirety of your message. Remember, no rabbit chasing in this neck of the woods! Stay focused on the main thing, or you could end up in the weeds far from the text you are preaching.

Some Texts Don't Need an Overload of Secondary Texts

You shouldn't feel compelled to add every verse you find in your research in the sermon. I've known some preachers that give an abundance of supporting Scriptures in their sermon, and it seems like they're just trying to convince their audience that they really did their homework! But cross-referencing lots of texts could confuse the listener and extend the message beyond the capacity of the listener.

Let's return to the old adage, "Keep the main thing the main thing." There have been times when I spent more time trying to figure out what needs to be left out of the sermon

Cross-referencing lots of texts could confuse the listener and extend the message beyond the capacity of the listener.

than what should be added. This is an important process. Don't waste the listeners' attention span. Separate the good from the best. C. H. Spurgeon said it like this: "Brevity is a virtue within the reach of all of us; do not let us lose the opportunity of gaining the credit which it brings. If you ask me how you may shorten your sermons, I should say, study them better. Spend more time in the study that you may need less in the pulpit. We are generally longest when we have least to say" (Lectures to my Students).[12]

Phase 3: Study the Languages

Perhaps the original language is difficult for you. If so, I want to press you to make this a part of your preparation. We have so many tools, books, and scholars. All of these can guide you through this no matter the place you are

---

12. Charles Spurgeon, *Lectures to My Students* (Peabody, MA: Hendrickson Publishers, 2010).

with your knowledge of Greek, Aramaic, and Hebrew. It's truly a pleasure and an adventure to plumb the depths of these ancient languages. The original languages do two main things: they will provide depth and clarity. You will invite your audience into a deeper meaning of even the most familiar verses.

When you study the original languages, you open up tools of understanding that you can't find anywhere else. The original languages not only expose you to greater meanings, they transport you into the time and culture that the Word was originally written.

The preacher who studies the original languages can also be better prepared to defend the Bible as an apologist. Martin Luther points this out: "A simple preacher (it is true) has so many clear passages and texts available through translations that he can know and teach Christ, lead a holy life, and preach to others. But when it comes to interpreting Scripture, and working with it on your own, and disputing with those who cite it incorrectly, he is unequal to the task; that cannot be done without languages."[13]

Warnings: Share these findings—but not all of them. Some pastors become narcissistic in their presentation when they overly communicate the meanings of words. Don't fall into the trap of flouting your research to make yourself look smart when there are people who are listening to get a Word from God. Remember, "we preach not ourselves" (2 Corinthians 4:5). Often I like to disarm the audience with a little self-depreciating humor when I share a Greek word. I'll say the word and then before the explanation, I'll say, "Now y'all need to listen close because I don't know but about two Greek words." Sometimes adding humor will let them know that while I am sharing something intellectually

13. From Hans H. Hillerbrand, *The Annotated Luther, Volume 5: Christian Life in the World* (Minneapolis, MN: Fortress Publishing, 2017) p. 264.

challenging, I'm still just a preacher who desire the focus to be on the message and not the messengers. Lord, help us all if the messenger overshadows the message.

Also, don't run right by the little words in the text. Look out for those words that seem small but have tremendous power. For instance, one of my favorite words in John 3:16 is the word *so*. It's easy to just look over a two-letter word, but this two-letter word makes all the difference. I can say I love the Tennessee Vols, ice cream, and a thousand other things, but in John 3:16, that "so" adds depth and width to the word. I like to say, "God sssssssssssso loved the world!" Sometimes a little word makes a big difference. Don't ignore them.

Phase 4: Use Correct and Compelling Commentaries

I'd begin with verse-by-verse commentaries written by theologians whose respect for the inerrant Word of God is obvious. In other words, drink from a pure cistern.

Why use verse-by-verse commentaries? The primary reason I use them is simple. During this phase of preparation, I want to zoom in on the precise meaning and purpose of each Scripture. I'm not looking at the big picture; I want to get into the details of exactly what the verse means to theologians I respect and trust. I'll be the first to tell you that God put me on this earth to preach the Word and win people for Jesus. Respected voices of theologians and ministers in the form of biblical commentaries will get me there faster. You'll discover different points of view as you utilize commentaries. Opening a commentary is opening up a virtual convocation of saints of old, theologians, Spirit-filled pastors, and creative communicators. You will receive a wide palette of perspectives that will open your heart to new aspects of the stories and precepts of the Bible. When I have a number of commentaries opened up on my desk and laptop computer, it's like I have a cadre of saints looking over my shoulder as I prepare. Who doesn't want that?

Phase 5: Make Good Use of Inspirational Resources Based on Scripture

I'd describe this as a warming-up phase for my preparation. I enjoy the language and style of writers like Adrian Rogers, W. A. Criswell, Chuck Swindoll, Oswald Chambers, Charles Stanley, Max Lucado, and other writers that populate the shelves of my study. These writers help me understand different ways to tell the amazing story of God. Many times, the pages I read from these writers are read for my own spiritual growth, but because they are such great writers, their illustrations, explanations, and stories burn themselves into my memory, and the Lord reminds me of them as I prepare sermons months after my first reading.

Here's an illustration of inspirational writing from Charles Stanley when considering the life and book of Daniel:

> *When I think of focus, I think of many instances in the Bible. One of the primary ones is Daniel in the lion's den. So the Bible says he slept with the lions all night. If he had been focused on lions he wouldn't have been sleeping. He would be over in the corner down somewhere hoping they wouldn't see him or something. And it brings me back to one of my favorite illustrations where God just did something for me in one of the most difficult times in my life. It probably was up to the very top. And this lady came to see me. And she said, I want you to have lunch with me then I want to take you up to my apartment and show you something. She was about 70 something and I was about 30 something, so I felt pretty safe. We ate lunch. I went to see her. I was going through a very*

difficult time at church. They were doing their best to try to get rid of me.

So she walked in and said, I want to show you something. She then showed me this picture of Daniel in the lion's den. She said, now son, I want you to tell me what you see. I said, well, and I can still remember looking at the picture. This lion over here looking up. This one looking down. I saw the bones. So I thought of everything this little lady would possibly think about it. She said do you see anything else. I said no. She said, if you notice, and the picture had all these lions and Daniel had his hands behind him looking at a ray of light. She said, what I want you to see is Daniel didn't have his eyes on the lions but on God. It was like God hugged me that day. Because from that moment on, all of my fears disappeared. All of my uncertainties and a lot of other things probably disappeared because she got my focus right.[14]

This is just one simple example of inspirational writing that speaks into the power of God's Word and the ancient story of a saint under fire. This book could neither catalogue nor contain the number of inspirational voices that are readily available to enhance the power of God's Word.

If we don't understand the truth of each verse we read, we will unintentionally avoid applying the message and God's ultimate purpose for Scripture.

One other note: If we don't understand the truth of each verse we read, we will unintentionally avoid applying the message and God's ultimate purpose for Scripture. It's true that by isolating a few verses, you can justify almost anything. But the truth is found in the whole counsel of God (Acts 20:27).

14. https://sermons.love/charles-stanley/1482-charles-stanley-wavering-faith.html

It's the most important truth we will ever declare, so let's not wander aimlessly through Scripture like a waiting, confused husband in the ladies' department of Dillard's, holding his wife's purse. All good husbands know that feeling of disorientation. Don't let that feeling recur on Sundays. Invest time in the text before you stand behind the pulpit. You'll have confidence, boldness, and direction.

In this chapter, we've considered how we invest in the text. Is this the end of our preparation? No. Not in the least. In chapter three: Maximize the Message, we'll move through the process of preparing a clear message, drawing from our personal experiences with God through the power of storytelling. And in chapter five, we'll consider the style and strategy for leading to the most important part of the craft of preaching—extending the invitation.

SUMMARY: INVEST IN THE TEXT

- Gumbo and the gospel—it's all in the Word
- Handle Scripture with holy care
- Scripture is the thrust of the message
- Easy steps:
  - » Read the text thoroughly
  - » Cross-reference your text with Scripture
  - » Study the languages
  - » Use correct and compelling commentaries
  - » Use good inspirational resources

JOURNAL THIS

1. How is the Bible shaping your heart today?

2. What study skills and commitments do you need to be a better student of the Word?

3

MAXIMIZE THE MESSAGE

"The whole process of sermon preparation, from beginning to end, was excellently summed up by an African American preacher who said, 'First I reads myself full, next I thinks myself clear, next I prays myself hot, and then I let go.'"
—*John Stott*

After I read the Scripture from the pulpit, I pray this prayer. It's a declaration and a request: "Lord, I pray that You'll just dismiss me, and You'd preach to us today. Move me out of the way." It's not liturgy. It's not a pleasant proverb of false humility. We've got to realize that the best thing we can do to maximize the Word is to minimize ourselves as preachers. God has a Word for everybody listening. We are all in different places. As I scan the auditorium where I preach, I realize that there are a thousand backstories, failures, questions, doubt, hurts, and fears behind the faces of the people staring back at me. My mother used to tell me, "Remember that over half of your people are hurting." There's more than a chance that somebody in your worship center (or church's stream) is at a breaking point.

- There's a husband that is struggling with internet pornography all the while wondering if his marriage will survive.

- There's a child who is so beaten down by bullying and depression that he wonders if he can go back to school tomorrow.

- There's a single mom who is doing everything she can to just put one foot in front of the other.

- There's a legalist who believes that he can make it to heaven on the coattails of his own religious resume.

- There's a teenager who has been fed a pack of lies by a science teacher and is wondering if there is even a God out there.

- There's a man who desperately turns to alcohol as a painkiller but is slowly discovering the painkiller is a man killer.

These people, whether they realize it consciously or not, are looking for a word from Almighty God. This is the place we're in right now. People are desperate for a word. "We would see Jesus" (John 12:21 KJV). They aren't interested in what Roc Collins has to say. They're interested in what *God* has to say! If we want to see God knock the doors down and rescue the weary, hopeless, wandering, questioning, and spiritually hungry congregation bound by the chains of their own sin and uncertainty, we have to maximize the message. Here are eight key disciplines every preacher must cultivate in order to maximize the message.

If we want to see God knock the doors down and rescue the weary, hopeless, wandering, questioning, and spiritually hungry congregation bound by the chains of their own sin and uncertainty, we have to maximize the message.

1. BEGIN WITH THE BIBLE

There are many preachers who come with pretty platitudes and pie-in-the-sky proclamations, but that's not where Jesus does His work. He's in the arena. He's striding toward the lost and the hopeless, muddling in the mire of a myriad of deceptions. The message *must* be maximized because we know that "faith comes by hearing, and hearing by the word of God" (Romans 10:17). What was Paul talking about when he wrote those words in Romans? Simple. *Preaching.* It never ceases to amaze me that God chose the media of preaching for soul winning, for reconciliation, for reproof, for instruction and guidance, for reprimand when necessary, and for training people in what is righteous.

God seems to prefer word-of-mouth more than any other media known to man. Looking back through history, we can see how radio succeeded in getting the preached Word of God around the globe—to remote villages and into countries that would not otherwise allow God's Word to be spoken. As technology expanded, so did man's ability to continue to spread the Word. Today we see the way social media is impacting our lives and our cultures in unimaginable ways. Through the heartbreaking coronavirus pandemic of 2020, pastors began to see a sudden spike in influence. A fellow pastor in our state shared a common experience: "My church runs fifty on a good Sunday, and we had over five hundred views of my sermon online!"

Has there ever been a greater need and opportunity to win the world for Jesus? Emphatically, no! And yet, with all the marvelous technology available to us, God hasn't changed His method. He transforms lives through anointed, passionate, prayer-saturated preaching.

The Word of God is alive! The Apostle Paul told his young friend Timothy that "All Scripture is inspired by God" (2 Timothy 3:16 NRSV). In New Testament Greek language, the word from this verse is Θέο-Πνέυμος, which literally translates to "God-breathed." Our Bible is not a collection of sayings and quips designed to make us feel good or to point our moral compasses in the best direction possible.

Hardly. The Word of God is not some dead artifact, thin-leaf paper with printer's ink from Grand Rapids, Michigan, or Nashville, Tennessee. It's animated grace.

No other literary work in the history of man has ever made such a claim. Perhaps that's why there are over five billion copies in over seven hundred languages of God's Word. It's alive. It's 783,137 words of power, purpose, and perfection.

A prison chaplain friend of mine told me a story about an encounter he had many years ago when he was just beginning his ministry at the Atlanta Federal Penitentiary. He said one night when the inmates had been recalled and his shift was over, he was walking toward the main building when he struck up a conversation with an older inmate.

"You must be the new chaplain. How are you doing?" the inmate asked.

"I'm fine, thanks. And you?"

"Not bad for an old man," the inmate said, adjusting the knitted kufi on his head. "Heard you in chapel today."

"You did?" replied the chaplain, surprised.

"Yeah. I grew up in a Christian house. I still like to go to the services now and again." He paused for a long moment and then continued. "Chaplain, I'm a Muslim now. And I have read the Quran several times, but . . ."

"But?" the chaplain replied.

"Well, that's just it, Chaplain. Like I said, I've read the Quran and I've read the Bible, and . . . well, the Bible *speaks* to me!"

"Not the Quran?" the chaplain asked.

"No," the inmate said. "Only the Bible."

There are many words that you can live by, but only God gives you a Word by which you can live! Because the Word of God is alive!

- *Preaching is not a speech.* The world is filled with rhetoric and talking heads.

- *Preaching is not editorializing.* We have news outlets for every political leaning.

- *Preaching is not entertainment.* Our culture is entertained to death.

- *Preaching is not self-help.* There's only One who can truly help.

- *Preaching IS a message from God being delivered by His preacher to His people.*

It's best stated in the book of Hebrews: "For the word of God is living and powerful, and sharper than any two-edged sword, piercing even to the division of soul and spirit, and of joints and marrow, and is a discerner of the thoughts and intents of the heart" (Hebrews 4:12).

This is what God entrusts to those whom He calls to preach. He entrusts us with His Word. His living and active Word! And that's why it is so important that the preacher understand what his role is in God's plan. The preacher must always remember that the message is not from him but from God. More accurately, the message is from God, through you, and to His people—the church. Notice that it comes *through* you and not *from* you. Some say the message is the messenger. Although character and example are vital, the truth is it doesn't have anything to do with the messenger. It's always been about the message.

Now, in order to fully maximize the message, it is imperative to know what God desires for you to deliver. Without seeking God's heart and what He desires His people to hear, your sermon will sound flat and lifeless. When you start with prayer and invest in the text, your message becomes incarnational. It's not about you. You have been dismissed. God takes over. And if it becomes about you, then you are just a few steps from ruin and vanity.

Avoid starting with a topic and cherry-picking Scripture to back up your thesis. Start with the Word, and the thesis writes itself. I've found that so many times when I begin preparation for a message, I study Scripture and the Holy Spirit begins to reveal truths I never expected before my preparation began. A phrase or a word pops out of the pages, and though I've read the passage many times, what's revealed is fresh and exciting. It's then, on an ordinary Tuesday, that I wish to God it was Sunday! This is what keeps a fire in me. Every encounter in personal, prayerful preparation becomes an adventure. I say, "Lord, I've read this a thousand times. What will You show me this time?"

Outside of this adventurous process with the Father, the message is simply an opinion from someone who can string some ideas together and call it a "sermon." But if it's in tune with God's heart, then behind that sermon is an unlimited power waiting to be unleashed on hearts that long for life-changing truth. Even a heart that is wandering or actively fleeing can recognize the Master's voice when it calls. And that is what can be accomplished when the man of God speaks the Word of God straight from the heart of God.

Once you know the message that God wants you to preach, and you have the Scripture from which you will prepare your sermon, it is time to compile all you can in relation to that message. In other words, use whatever you have at your disposal to illustrate the message. Keep in mind the goal is to have sufficient information for the hearers to be able not only to understand but to fully grasp the message God has given you.

2. MAXIMIZE TOOLS

There's really no excuse, guys. The mechanics and tools of preparation have never been so available. Can you imagine the Apostle Paul with a Macbook Pro? Can you wrap your head around his use of email? Can you imagine Charles Spurgeon on YouTube or George Whitfield mentoring pastors on Zoom? It's fun to think about, isn't it? But in God's providence, we have tools that people a century ago could only dream about. That's why I say, there's no excuse. We have more than enough to assist us in preparation.

I was teaching homiletics in Waspan, Nicaragua, some years ago. There were forty pastors of all ages that had gathered in this small northern village to learn more about preaching. Somewhere in my introduction, I asked how many of them had any resources other than their Bible. Only two men raised their hands. My heart broke when I thought of the books and computer resources that I had in my office. I was glad to tell them that their Bible was enough. But at the same time, I was reminded of how blessed we are with resources to help us prepare and present the precious Word of God. With the amount of resources at our disposal, we should never stand to deliver God's Word without being fully prepared. We don't have a lack of resources but often a lack of resolve to complete the task that God has given us. May God help us to always be prepared.

3. VET THE VOICES

Today, it's not a matter of finding tools. Tools and resources are ubiquitous. The question is, *What tools will you use?* We must use discernment to find gospel-centered resources that are in total compliance with the Word of God if we are to rightly divide it.

To begin with, places for finding sermon illustration material is only limited by your own imagination. But first and foremost, the absolute best place to start is within Scripture itself. In Latin, it is referred to as *analogia scriptorium*, or "the analogy of the Scriptures." In our modern English it could be described as, "letting Scripture interpret Scripture." For example, I've heard sermons on the crucifixion of Jesus as recorded in the Gospels which were accompanied by vivid, clinical accounts of what happens physically to a person during that particular act of execution. It was fascinating and disturbing at the same time. But when you compare the crucifixion in the Gospels with what is recorded in Psalm 22, well, it was like I was seeing it through the eyes of God. In actuality, I was seeing it through the eyes of Scripture, and it was nothing short of powerful!

4. PAINT THE PICTURE

Life is stuffed with literature and stories that will help you dynamically express the truths of God's Word. As I said before, there are no limits to your resources, including the daily news report, nature, sports, and life itself. Considering how intertwined God is with His creation, it's no wonder He reveals Himself in myriad places.

In a series of sermons I once heard on the believer's spiritual armor (Ephesians 6:10-17), the preacher drove home Paul's command to the believer to "stand firm, ...having shod your feet with the preparation of the gospel of peace." He thoroughly described the sandals worn by soldiers in the Roman army which had hob-nailed soles, allowing them a better means of digging in and standing their ground in battle, not unlike our modern-day sports cleats. His illustration blew me away. He recounted a championship football game that basically came down to a goal line stand by the defensive squad. The offensive team pushed and pushed toward the end zone. First down. Second down. Third down. Finally, fourth down. And they needed a touchdown since a field goal would not have given them enough points for the win. It was up to the defensive players to hold their ground and prevent the touchdown. And they did. They dug in with the cleats on the soles of their feet and held their ground.

Do your very best to find appropriate, meaningful illustrations to help your message come alive in the minds of the hearers. Illustrations complement the task of the preacher to proclaim the message from God's heart in a way in which it can be received in the hearts of His people today. Developing the art of succinct storytelling can be a powerful means to bring relevant meaning to the truth from Scripture.

Dr. R. G. Lee was one of, if not *the* greatest preacher of the twentieth century. His ability to speak descriptively was amazing. Once, while describing a letter he received from someone who was quite vulgar, he stated, "To find a good word in the letter was like finding a gardenia in a garbage dump." His ability to paint a picture with His words was a unique gift from God.

At the same time, he was a well-studied man. We must never forget the importance of giving ourselves to continual study and preparation, not just for a message but to improve as a communicator.

S. M. Lockridge, another legendary voice of the pulpit, spent time not only telling a story well, he also used language akin to poetry to inspire. Notice the power of his words:

> *We must never forget the importance of giving ourselves to continual study and preparation, not just for a message but to improve as a communicator.*

I'm trying to say He died. But I don't like to say He died, I like to rush on and say that He was buried *in a borrowed tomb*. That used to bother me. The one who holds the waters in the hull of His hand, meets out the heavens with a speck, comprehends the dust and weighs the mountains and their scale and the hills in the balance. The one who walked on nothing and with a gesture of his hands, words were formed. Scooped out the seas with the palm of his hand. Dug deep the gorges, piled up the hills and, propped up the mountains by his will. The moon and stars lean on his arm. Being buried in a borrowed tomb. While he wasn't going to stay there long . . ."

Stories and illustrative words infuse our sermons with dynamic grace. They communicate with power. After all, we are communicators, but we are communicators of the glorious gospel of Jesus Christ. As one of my preacher friends says, "Paint that picture!"

5. READ EVERY DAY

For most preachers, it's a battle to carve out time to read. The old adage is true for preachers: "If you're through reading, you're through." A preacher must prime the pump. When you read, you open a spiritual treasure chest of men who have gone before us and the men that walk beside us today. Let's get real. How much time do you spend reading when you compare it to the time you spend watching ESPN or binging on the news? If that question makes you nervous, you might want to dust off the top shelf of your library.

I have to confess—this is difficult. It's so much easier to let entertainment flow over us than to actively engage in a book. Every hour you spend reading improves your preaching by 23 percent. OK . . . I made that up, but you get the point. Devour God's Word first, then dive into supplementary reading and find the "off" button on your remote.

6. USE YOUR STORY

Your story is powerful! There's nobody in this world who has the same story with God that you do. We share universal experiences but unique stories. Think about it. This is what makes your story powerful and transforming. When you share from your personal experiences, you are doing several things:

- *You let the audience in on who you really are.* The power in your message is always God's power. His message is always primary. But your story makes the power of God personal. Some pastors fill their sermons with other people's experiences. That's good. But do you know what's better? Your experience. It's why we call it "testimony." Your story isn't hearsay. It's first-person testimony that would stand stronger in the court of law than you sharing somebody else's experience with God. It's like that old poem written by that famous preacher, Brother Unknown:

  > *What you are speaks so loud that the world can't hear what you say;*
  > *They're looking at your walk, not listening to your talk,*
  > *They're judging from your actions every day.*
  > *Don't believe you'll deceive*
  > *By claiming what you've never known*
  > *They'll accept what they see and know you to be,*
  > *They'll judge from your life alone.*

  Don't have a story to tell? Perhaps you need to go out and live one! For instance, if you are preaching on evangelism this Sunday, you might want to make sure you start a number of gospel conversations before Saturday night rolls around (just sayin'). It's not hard. Go share with the cashier at the grocery store during your next milk run and you've got your story.

- *You make the message practical.* People are wanting to know how the gospel is played out in your life. This allows them a glimpse into how they can live out the gospel in their lives also. If all you give them is high-minded principles and no practical stories of how it works in the real world, you're aren't giving them the leg-up they need to make the changes they need in their lives.

- *You make the message relatable.* For some reason, the old myth that the preacher is more holy and untouchable still survives. Your audience needs to relate to you as a person. This is one of the key dynamics of the incarnation. Jesus came down in human skin so that He could embody the message of the gospel. He took a huge step closer to humanity. It's intimacy. We should do likewise. Stories help us do that.

- When I preach about death, I can draw from the wellspring of grief I've experienced from the loss of my father and other family members and friends I've loved. When my dad died in 1986, I was eighteen years old, and I realized how badly I was hurting. I also realized how badly my mother and my sister were hurting. Through experience, I came to realize that people all grieve differently. My mother grieved as a wife. My sister grieved as a daughter. I grieved as a son. Our experiences were different. We grieved differently, but we grieved together. This is the power of story. Although we are unique in our suffering, for that moment in the story, people who knew nothing about my experience are transported into that sacred space of grief that we all stand in at one time or another.

  Years later my sister died after a long battle with cancer. Six months later, I got called to the home where a lady was about to die. Her brother, who was a member of my church, came in, and when he saw me, he just hugged me and said, "I know that you know how I feel." This is the power of our story. Our stories are unique. But our stories are uniquely relatable.

I've learned over the years that a story is more relatable than any Gallup Poll result or statistic I've discovered.

- *You become vulnerable.* Sometimes we think that vulnerability is a bad thing, but in the pulpit, you need to let the vulnerability flag fly! And don't just tell them of the victories, show them your scars. Remember that the gospel is about a wounded Healer. Vulnerability is uncomfortable, but ultimately it has tremendous power in the Lord's hands.

As you prepare to preach, the Holy Spirit will begin to bring experiences from your life into focus.

7. FINISH STRONG!

It's a part of almost every game. The final two minutes, the ninth inning, or the final turn are the most important. The same is true in preaching. You need to *bring it* in the final two or three minutes of your message.

There are two primary ingredients: passion and preparation. No preacher has ever meandered listlessly into a powerful conclusion that refuses to be forgotten. I believe that your *prayer-peration* is the key. I remember speaking to a group of pastors. My heart was so burdened for them. Many of the guys told me stories of upset deacons, family trials, discouragement, and controversy. I knew there were two words I wanted them to leave hearing: "Don't quit!" I felt it so strongly as if the Lord had placed those two words on my mind like a blinking light on the dash of my pickup. *Don't quit!* I knew this was important. I took the time to write down exactly what I wanted to say. I don't write out my sermons, but I often plan endings word for word because I know how important the final lap really is. The words came quickly:

Don't Quit!

Sometimes the road gets lonely and the friends are few.
Sometimes the burdens are heavy, and the trials seem to never end.
But Don't Quit!
When the frustration is high and the funds are low,
When the worship is dry and the "amen"s have dried up!
When the altar is empty and the baptismal waters are still,
Don't You Quit!
When the deacons are demanding, the naysayers are vocal, and staff is disgruntled.
When your wife is weary, your children are discouraged, and you are ready to throw in the towel!
Don't You Quit!
We serve a great God! Why, He can:
acquit the guilty
bless the burdened
calm the troubled waters
Don't You Quit—just trust the One who can:
diffuse the disgruntled
extinguish the fires of demons
give peace in the midst of the storm
I know it's tough, but Don't You Quit!
Our God can:
help the hurting
inspire the down-hearted and discouraged
justify the sinner
keep the saint
love the unlovable
and make a way where there is no way!
The road gets long, the valley is wide, but Don't You Quit!

The One who called you can:
nourish the soul
overcome any obstacle
provide every need
quiet the gossip and
revive the Spirit
Why, He can:
satisfy the longing of your heart
turn your night into day
use our weakness
visit with the hurting
work when no one else can
revive the exhausted and give zeal to the weary
Don't You Quit!
People are dying and going to hell.
Hatred is rampant.
Lies are being told as truth,
And Truth is called a lie.
But Don't you Quit!
Our God is still on the throne!
He still reigns!
His hand is still on the throttle!
Don't You Quit!
I know it's hard, I know you're tired, I know you feel
defeated!
But Don't You Quit!
One of these sweet days King Jesus is going to call us
home,
And we will rest from the battle in the sweet arms of
Jesus!
He will place a crown on our head as we join the throngs
in heaven and shout,
"Jesus is Lord, and it was worth it all!"

8. CAST THE NET

As you prepare to preach, begin with the end in mind. Every message you preach should be a call to action. You need to ask yourself, *How will God change people through this message?* If you don't have a strong call to action, you need to seriously ask yourself why you preach!

We always preach with an eye to transformation. As mentioned in chapter one, preachers need to ask the Father for the things only He can do. This seems like such a no-brainer, but in these times, it has to be said: *every sermon should end with a strong gospel invitation.* Forbid it to be so that we would preach without offering a lost soul the gift of eternal life. I want our marriages to be strong, and I'll preach on marriage, but what good is it if you help them figure out how to live in harmony on earth if their ultimate destination is hell? Every message we preach should lead everyone to change. We'll drill down on the gospel invitation in chapter six.

> *Every sermon should end with a strong gospel invitation. Forbid it to be so that we would preach without offering a lost soul the gift of eternal life.*

IT'S OUR TIME!

I know I have less days on earth to preach this message than yesterday. I think about that often. My grandfather was a preacher. He's in heaven now. My father was a preacher. He's there with him. They're enjoying the fruits of their labor in this glorious adventure called the gospel. It's my turn. I'm up to bat. And I'm not laying down any bunts. I'm swinging for the fences. I hope you are too.

SUMMARY: MAXIMIZE THE MESSAGE

- Begin with the Bible
- Maximize your tools
- Vet the voices
- Paint the picture
- Read every day
- Use your story
- Finish strong
- Cast the net

JOURNAL THIS

1. What hard experience have you been through that has shaped your preaching?

2. How will you guard your time to prepare with so many demands on your time?

3. What resources are you planning to invest in to improve your knowledge, skill, and preparation?

4

PREACH!
&
LEAVE IT ALL IN
THE PULPIT

"The pulpit is ever this earth's foremost part; all the rest comes in its rear; the pulpit leads the world. . . . Yes, the world's a ship on its passage out, and not a voyage complete; and the pulpit is its prow."
—*Herman Melville*

I remember those crisp, fall Friday nights in North Carolina—the smell of the popcorn, the excitement of hearing the band warm up and the crowd filing into the high school stadium. I remember our coach's steely-eyed stare as we gathered around for the last word before the biggest game of the year:

> Leave it all on the field. Don't back up. Press them at every turn. Let them know that you are going

to be in their face on every down, no matter what happens. I don't care what the scoreboard says, you just keep coming! I don't want you to waste a second of this opportunity we have. Some of you seniors will remember what happens tonight for the rest of your lives. What story do you want to tell your kids ten years from now? Drive hard. Remember the fundamentals we've worked on since the first day of spring drills and summer two-a-days. Have each other's back like your life depended on it. If you leave it all on the field, you'll never regret it!

I'm older now, but I've transferred that clarion call from a simple high school football coach to Sunday morning. I've determined on any given Sunday to leave it all in the pulpit. I'm not going to back up, settle for normal, or waste an opportunity. Just like the scene in *Dead Poets' Society*, with the students gathering around the pictures of students from long ago, I hear my Teacher, the Holy Spirit, say, *Seize the day! Make your message extraordinary!* I want to preach every sermon as if it were my last, because there's always a chance it might be!

One evening after I preached at a pastor's conference, my good friend Stephen Rummage pulled me aside and said, "You are the only preacher I know that approaches preaching like an athletic event." Oh, to God that my passion for the gospel would always be approached with conviction, fervor, and intensity!

At the time of this writing, I'm sitting at my house exhausted after four video meetings, a flood of emails, and several phone calls to pastors like myself. It's been eight weeks since I've stood before a live and in-person congregation. It's been the most difficult time in my career. I've preached to my wife, my sons, my dog, Louis, the milk jug, and the peanut butter jar! Talk about a stir-crazy preacher. I embody the term. God didn't wire me for "shelter in place." I don't think I'll ever take preaching for granted again. But when I do return, I want to leave it all in the pulpit!

In this chapter, I want to both instruct you and inspire you to go hard, go strong, and hold nothing back. We'll start with a little homespun advice.

EXTEND YOUR ENERGY

If you'll allow me, I'd like to give you some Momma advice. You probably know what I mean by *Momma advice*. That's just the practical, prudent, and important things you need to do. It's not flowery, metaphysical, or proverbial. It's like Joe Friday: "Just the facts."[15] So here it goes.

Get to bed early Saturday night. Be careful about what you put before your eyes before you go to bed. Let your mind rest in the Word. By this time, it's probably too late to prepare.

Watch what you eat. In other words, take care of God's temple the night before you preach. Sunday's coming, and you want to be at your best.

Make sure the air is clear with your wife. There's nothing more excruciating than preaching from the pulpit when your wife isn't happy. Protect, nurture, and bless the bond you have with her.

Stay away from meetings. I've had those Sunday mornings when I'm called to a meeting before Sunday school and I become so distracted by the subject that I walk up to the pulpit with an emotional battery life of fifteen percent. I can hear the Lord scolding me. *You had* one job*! I gave you one job today!*

And finally…

Avoid those irregular people. They can wait for now. The last thing you need is to face the flesh-driven scorn of the sarcastic committee chairman who takes you on as his hobby.

---

15. Fictional character in "Dragnet."

It ain't worth it! At least not right before the instruments tune up in the sanctuary. (To tell you the truth, I don't think it's ever worth it!)

But most of all, rest in the Lord. Breathe. Worship. Sing. Live in the moment of the music before the message. You need to worship too.

I love Psalm 91. It's a go-to passage as I prepare for the Sunday battle. I especially love the beauty of the King James Version. Let it flow over you once again.

> *He that dwelleth in the secret place of the most High shall abide under the shadow of the Almighty. I will say of the Lord, He is my refuge and my fortress: my God; in him will I trust. Surely he shall deliver thee from the snare of the fowler, and from the noisome pestilence. He shall cover thee with his feathers, and under his wings shalt thou trust: his truth shall be thy shield and buckler. Thou shalt not be afraid for the terror by night; nor for the arrow that flieth by day; Nor for the pestilence that walketh in darkness; nor for the destruction that wasteth at noonday. A thousand shall fall at thy side, and ten thousand at thy right hand; but it shall not come nigh thee. Only with thine eyes shalt thou behold and see the reward of the wicked. Because thou hast made the Lord, which is my refuge, even the most High, thy habitation; There shall no evil befall thee, neither shall any plague come nigh thy dwelling. For he shall give his angels charge over thee, to keep thee in all thy ways. (vv. 1-11)*

I believe Sunday starts on Saturday night. I think my momma would agree!

INCREASE YOUR URGENCY

Richard Baxter, a preacher in the 1600s, said, "I preach as never sure to preach again, and as a dying man to dying men." I shout an "amen" through the halls of time to that statement. Pastor David Landreth pastored Long Hollow Church in Hendersonville, Tennessee, for many years. He was diagnosed with cancer but continued to preach and lead his church until the Lord called him home. The last year he was the pastor there, he saw over one thousand people profess Jesus Christ as Lord and follow Him in baptism. I remember talking to someone from the church and asking them about the mighty move of God. They echoed the words of Richard Baxter: "He was a dying man preaching to dying people."

While it was literally true in this situation, it is true in our situations too. We are dying men preaching to dying people, and Jesus is our only hope. Think about it. We aren't getting any younger. Nobody is. We are all stepping closer to the grave, if the Lord tarries.

We are dying men preaching to dying people, and Jesus is our only hope.

I believe every pastor must preach with urgency. When we stand in the pulpit, let's focus on the fact that everyone will make a decision about what they hear. Many listeners will decide not to decide. Just the thought of their indecision kindles a fire of urgency in my soul as I preach. As the old saying goes, *The only thing the devil has to do is to convince the lost soul that there is plenty of time.* I want to preach in such a way that nobody in the house, especially me, believes they have plenty of time.

As pastors, we are reminded of this on a consistent basis. We go to more funerals than anybody—other than the funeral director. Most of us are more conscious of the fragility of life because we spend a great deal of time speaking in front of dead people. On Sunday we speak before dead people also. There are some in the audience that sit in a state of spiritual rigor mortis. They are dead, dead, dead. At a funeral we memorialize the dearly departed. On Sundays we bring people to life. This time is precious, and it demands a sense of holy urgency.

My dad was my pastor, and when I was eighteen years old God called him home. When the day of the funeral came, I had nothing to preach, or so it seemed. I thought, *What was I thinking?* Looking back, I know what I was thinking. I was thinking that I loved my dad and wanted to say something. I scribbled a few notes that no one could read or possibly make any sense of but me. When I stood to speak, God's peace flooded my soul. I don't remember all I said, but I do remember the overwhelming presence of the Lord. My hurt and sadness in that moment was almost unbearable, but I would gladly return to that hurt just to experience the presence of the Holy Spirit's power as I did that day in 1986. Oh, to experience the power of the Holy Spirit when you are in God's pulpit!

AVOID DISTRACTIONS

From my early years of little league through high school, no matter what sport I played, I heard a common message from all my coaches. Whether it was on the diamond, the hardwood floor, or the gridiron, coaches would say it over and over. *Keep your eyes on the ball!* Don't look at the opponent's eyes. Don't second guess the play. Don't get distracted by the crowd, the banners, or the venue. Keep your eyes on the ball! We've all seen what happens when an athlete fails to keep his eyes on the ball.

- The football crashes off the back of the wide receiver's helmet in the end zone.

- The no-look pass ends up bouncing off the ear of the teammate.

- The baseball rolls slowly between the legs of the shortstop, while he's deciding where to throw the ball. It's embarrassing, especially if it happens on national television.

You can almost hear the eviscerating shouts of exasperated coaches and fellow players: *Keep your eyes on the ball!* No matter how many times a player enters the arena, forgetting the basics remains a threat to victory and excellence. I've thought about that phrase over the past few months. As Christ-followers and leaders, we must keep our eyes on the ball. We are often distracted, especially in the midst of this chaotic year like 2020. We have been surrounded by distractions and challenges that could easily sabotage our mission. As Yogi Berra would say, "We've got to keep the main thing the main thing."

> *We face many distractions. We must never forget that the main thing is the atoning sacrifice of Jesus and our compelling challenge to share the gospel.*

As preachers, we have been called to do eternal things, and we have enemies that crave our attention. The devil's minions are in the stands as we walk up to the line to shoot. They have signs, noise makers, and gestures galore. They jig around like the Duke cheering section in the Final Four, and they want to be noticed. It seems like they've been working overtime, doesn't it?

We face many distractions. We must never forget that the main thing is the atoning sacrifice of Jesus and our compelling challenge to share the gospel. Here's a short list of distractions all believers are facing today.

The Distraction of Politics

The right will never be right, the progressive will never progress, and the activist will never be activated without a focused view of God's glorious gift of salvation and a passion for fulfilling the Great Commission. We must keep our eyes on the ball. I believe there may be some that listen to their favorite news outlet more than they listen to the Word. There is only One person that can make sense of the mess we find ourselves in as a nation and as believers. We must focus on Him.

The Distraction of Prejudice

Our prejudice is our unwillingness to see every person as one created in the image of God. This can't happen. If we don't view people as image bearers, we aren't keeping our eyes on the ball. Racial reconciliation matters to God, and it should matter to us too. If we are unwilling to love radically and carefully listen, we will allow our own sinful prejudice to distract us from the ministry of reconciliation. We are to reconcile to others and be reconciled with God. We can't do one without the other. If the church can't rise above its own prejudice, nobody can.

The Distraction of Panic

We also contend with the fatal distraction of fear. We have feared disease, rioting, financial downturns, and an uncertain future. What happens when we are distracted by fear? We pull back. We circle the wagons of our savings and relationships. We fail to risk. The greatest antidote for fear is a relentless conviction to carry on, to love despite the consequences, and to give foolishly. God blesses this kind of foolishness. He adores it! It represents a trust that God is still on the throne, and we are keeping our eyes on the ball.

The Distraction of Passivity

The distraction of fear also wreaks havoc on our willingness to preach the gospel. We can become passive in our preaching. The enemy would have us see the opportunities for gospel proclamation decreasing. Our nation is becoming more and more Godless. We might be deceived into believing that it's worse than it's ever been. But let me remind you of a handful of believers in the first century. In less than a century, they went from living underground in caves and catacombs to the most dominate faith community in the span of a century. They were under far more persecution than we are today. They were cast into arenas of hungry lions, and yet they roared out the gospel with such passion that it turned the world upside-down. Would to God that we would not be distracted by our fears but rather be emboldened by our faith!

Jesus is at work. He is on the move, and *He's looking at the church*. He's challenging us to cast off those things that beset us—our pride, our prejudice, our fear, and our safety nets. Don't let these distractions cause you to take your eye off the ball. Don't fall. Don't fear. Don't faint.

DON'T WASTE YOUR TIME

Leaving it all on the field means putting first things first. Don't waste your allotted time to preach lost in insignificant words or stories that distract from the message. Avoid the temptation to make yourself the hero of every story or punchline. *Preach the Word!*

A pastor friend of mine tells this simple story of a member in his church who doesn't teach Sunday school or serve on a committee—he just fixes things. Though he's a typical middle-class, blue-collar worker, he gives with *extreme* generosity. If a kid couldn't afford camp, somehow this layman would find out and show up at the office with a check. His investment in the Kingdom won't be fully understood until the time we meet in glory. Every time someone would thank him, he'd graciously say, "Thank you. That's why I'm here." What's my point? If you've been called of God, remember: *That's why you're here!* Don't waste your time in the pulpit settling scores, impressing the deacons, telling humorous stories, or tinkering with flowery word pictures that have nothing to do with the message. *Preach the Word!* (Yes. I am screaming as I type.) If you are not doing this, you're just wasting time.

YOU ARE NOT ALONE

As you preach, ruminate on the fact that you are not alone in the process. The Holy Spirit is preaching alongside you. I don't know about you, but this excites me! We have power in our preaching when we are captured and controlled by the Holy Spirit's power. There have been times when people have come to me after I've preached and quote their favorite part of my message, and I think to myself, *I don't even remember saying that!* I think most seasoned preachers have shared that experience. I'd have to say the reason I don't remember it rests in the fact that I didn't say it. The Holy Spirit said it.

> *When we preach the Word, we disrupt people's lives. . . . Distant, disconnected fathers need a little disruption on Sunday morning. The sleeping church needs a disruption. The sanctimonious hypocrite needs disruption. The world groans with a desperate need for holy disruption.*

When we preach the Word, we disrupt people's lives. That sounds negative, but our society needs disruptions. Distant, disconnected fathers need a little disruption on Sunday morning. The sleeping church needs a disruption. The sanctimonious hypocrite needs disruption. The world groans with a desperate need for holy disruption. It's not enough for us to tiptoe through the status quo. When we preach, we have to filter our flesh—but not the Holy Spirit. The most courageous preachers I know will say anything God tells them to say without blinking an eye or worrying about the consequences. And that's difficult because everybody wants to be loved and esteemed. But in the end, you won't be judged by how many friends you have on Facebook or the number of good reviews you have on your YouTube page. You'll be rewarded by your faithfulness to preach the unvarnished, soul-saving Word of God.

Truth telling can be hard, but that's what we do. If you are not into truth telling, will you please resign from your church and take up a career selling timeshare vacations? We need men who are empowered by the Holy Spirit to speak truth into the lives of their people. King David had at least two outside truthtellers, and unlike many, he not only listened to them—he changed. One was the truth-telling prophet Nathan. He's the one that pointed his finger at David during the King's sordid affair with Bathsheba. He shared painful, gut-wrenching truth. David shares a second Truthteller with us: God Himself. Everybody needs both: a man of God to speak in an audible voice to our souls and the Word of God that whispers in a still small voice. Truth has to be our friend. Without it, there's no real growth. As preachers, our role cannot be diminished. But it will be marginalized and minimized if we don't speak difficult truth.

LISTEN FOR THE "AUDIBLES"

When we leave it all in the pulpit, we have to be sure we listen for the audibles. Audibles have become a mainstay in football over the years. The quarterback surveys the field and notices the defense is stacking the line, the cornerbacks are subtly stepping closer to the linemen, and you hear the quarterback shout to his teammates, "Kill, Kill, Kill!" Everybody knows he's about to change the play. The Holy Spirit sometimes changes the play before the message, during the message, or even during the invitation. There have been times during the invitation when I see that God is moving in a way I didn't expect, and I hear an audible. There are times the Lord prompts my mind to address a spiritual issue in the middle of the sermon, and it's so evident to me that I have to address it. God has called an audible!

I love Peyton Manning and so enjoyed watching him play football. Through his days at The University of Tennessee and his days in the NFL, he was like a chess master on the field. He played with the fire of a field general. I remember him yelling, "Omaha, Omaha," when he would call out the audible. He would call an audible because he had seen with his own eyes where there was an opening, and he knew the play that would move the team down the field. The Holy Spirit calls an audible when He sees the work of the enemy and knows how to move His people forward. He knows the message and the people more than you do. Listen to Him!

I have often stood preaching and the Holy Spirit is speaking to me so fast that I can hardly get it out fast enough. He knows more than I do, He loves deeper than I do, and He knows who is there and what they need to hear. Listen to Him, and even as Mary the mother of Jesus said at the wedding of Cana, "Whatever He says, do it!"

One other side note: audibling your whole sermon sometimes but very rarely occurs. Be wary of the impulse to scrap your entire message just before worship. I believe God blesses a well-prepared message. There may be a national crisis, a death, or a church tragedy such as a termination or a brewing conflict in the church that leads you to throw out the playbook, but those times are few and far between. Test the Spirit. If you feel that impulse often, you might be confusing the still small voice of God with the shifting voice of your flesh. Also, remember that you are a part of a team that works together to weave the music, the media, and the message. Shifting the sermon frequently damages the Spirit of your worship team.

LET GOD SPEAK TO YOUR SOUL TOO

John Stott got it right when he said, "The best sermons we ever preach to others are those we have first preached to ourselves."[16] I heard a story of a preacher who preached the message God called him to preach. He called his associate pastor to the front for the invitation, and on the third stanza he turned to that associate pastor for prayer and rededication. Now that's preaching. When you are so convicted by the Word of God and you are so moved that you can dismiss yourself from your own platform to receive a touch of renewal. That's one boomerang message!

You will never be able to preach about things you don't know about. For instance, I can't preach John 3:16 if I have a hard time putting my name in the "whosoever." Unless I can say, "For God so loved Roc . . . ," I have no business preaching that verse. Just between us two, I love the way that sounds. There's a world that's looking for love in all the wrong places. (I know it sounds like an old country song.) They are starving to death for love. If you don't know that God *so* loves you, how can you preach the love of God?

It was November 3rd, 1995. I was at Forrest General Hospital in Hattisburg, Mississipppi. Earlier that day, Jeralyn called me and said, "It is time to go to the hospital. Our baby is coming." I knew for nine months that it was going to be a boy. I told everybody, "It's a boy." And that night, God gave us a boy. It was just overwhelming! I slipped out of the room and walked down the hall to call my mother who was in East Tennessee. And I said, "Mother, I just want you to know you have a grandson."

Of course she was so excited. We talked for a while, and then I said I've got to go. My mother said, "Before you go, I have to tell you something." I listened as she composed herself. She said, "Now you know how much I love you." The reality was almost too much to take in. It was a holy moment. But she had one more thing she had to say. It remains with me to this day: "Now you know how much God loves you."

I believe that's the same way it is for preachers. Until you experience and believe completely that God so loved, you'll never be able to preach it.

16. John Stott, *Between Two Worlds* (Grand Rapids, MI: William B. Eerdmans Publishing Company, 2017).

FINISH WITH A FLURRY!

Your last impression is your greatest impression; therefore, your last words are your most important words. This is why I often write my conclusion rather than just creating a few bullet points as prompts. Let's run with purpose through the goal line instead of stumbling in and landing awkwardly on our backs.

The sermons I remember most are the ones that shake the soul. S. M. Lockridge was a master at this. He'd use rhythm and artful repetition to drive home the motherload of the message. Use the conclusion of the sermon to move your audience toward radical change and transformational decisions. Give your people a shot of inspiration. Allow them to see themselves in the story. Make it personal. Don't let them off the hook! This is a cynical, brutal, barren world for believers these days. Sometimes when preachers spend too much time in the study, they forget how bad it is in the real world. They've got to know how your message can breathe life into their bone-dry surroundings. Challenge, encourage, delight, and inspire them. They need to look up! And let me stop right here and encourage you, pastor, to look up too!

I know the task is great but *look up*!
I know the burdens are heavy and the hours are long.
I know the adversaries seem to increase, and it seems there are more against you than are for you.
There is little to no encouragement.
Prayer time has become stale and lifeless.
The study is challenging, and there is no fire in the pulpit.
But I came to tell you,
Look up—look up, man of God . . .
God is still on His throne, and He knows where you are.

The enemy cannot destroy you because he has been defeated.

Our Lord still has a plan for you and work for you to do.

The chains of defeat are falling off, and the chorus of victory is tuning up.

The dread of facing the enemy . . .

is being replaced with the delight of victory in Jesus.

The naysayers are going to nay.

The dissenters are going to dissent.

The gossipers are going to gossip.

The haters are going to hate.

But Thou, O Lord, are a shield for me—

You are my protection and my provision.

You are my strength and my sustenance.

You are my help and my hope.

You are my bounty and my blessing.

You are my power and my portion.

You are my glory, and in You and You alone will I glory . . .

So, *no* more defeat. Today I am determined to trust in Thou, O Lord!

For Thou, O Lord, art a shield for me and the lifter of my head.

"I will lift up mine eyes unto the hills, from whence cometh my help, My Help cometh from the Lord which made Heaven and Earth!" (Psalm 121:1-2 KJV)

Man of God, look up!

PREACH IT AND LEAVE IT

I believe that after you finish preaching well, you can expect to be mentally, emotionally, and physically exhausted. Why? Because you left it all in the pulpit. You will have leveraged every resource you have, including a few that you don't. Why do I even want to mention that? Two reasons:

1. First of all, you might think you are doing it wrong to be that depleted. I would respond by saying you are doing it just right. You have toiled under the yoke of proclamation. It's the most important message known to man since Adam and Eve limped shamefully out of Eden. If you completed the task in a slipshod, laissez-faire, "that'll do" manner, then you're not crossing the goal line—you're fumbling the ball.

2. The second reason I mention this is so that you allow yourself recovery time. It's well documented that a muscle needs anywhere from twenty-four to forty-eight hours to repair and rebuild, and working it again too soon simply leads to tissue breakdown instead of building. This is why veteran preachers always say, "Never resign on Monday morning." You need time to recover. Your body needs it. Your soul needs it. Pastors, don't make the mistake of allowing exhaustion from the heart-racing battle you experienced on Sunday cause you to run for the hills to escape that conniving Jezebel on Monday. Take time to rest and recover.

You might think you are doing it wrong to be that depleted. I would respond by saying you are doing it just right. You have toiled under the yoke of proclamation.

This is why it's ill advised to have committee meetings or counseling sessions on Sunday afternoon at 12:30. Be with your family. Like the deep-sea diver, surface slowly and decompress. You'll need it. You left it all in the pulpit.

SUMMARY: PREACH! & LEAVE IT ALL IN THE PULPIT

- Extend your Energy
- Increase your Urgency
- Don't waste your time
- You are not alone
- Listen for the Audibles
- Let God speak to your soul
- Finish with a Flurry
- Preach it and Leave it

JOURNAL THIS

1. Who do you preach to weekly that needs a clear word from God?

2. How do you prepare physically for preaching?

3. When is the last time you fasted?

4. What's been your biggest regret about your preaching so far?

5

EXTEND THE INVITATION

"The Church exists for nothing else but to draw men into Christ, to make them little Christs. If they are not doing that, all the cathedrals, clergy, missions, sermons, even the Bible itself, are simply a waste of time. God became Man for no other purpose."
—*C. S. Lewis*

You've heard the old adage, "The worst day of fishing is better than the best day at work." I don't agree. It seems pointless to endlessly cast, reel in, change lures, navigate the boat between the stumps in the water, suffer under the sweltering heat, and wait patiently without anything to show for it. If I'm going to fish, I want some action. Don't you? In the same way, one of the most discouraging things a man of God can do is to preach Sunday after Sunday with little change, no decisions, and no movement during the invitation. But just like a patient fisherman who spends his day languishing with little to show, we continue to preach.

I'm not a big fisherman, but I have heard stories of guys who fish all day in legendary hotspots around the banks, in the places they've caught the six pounders the year before—and then before the sun creeps lower on the horizon and just before they troll back to the boat ramp, they get their first hit.

Then another and another. The excitement of finding a new hotspot is exhilarating, and it just makes them want more.

I know that feeling as a preacher. I've preached my heart out in a revival and languished desperately to see God begin to move, and then suddenly heaven's floodgates open and God brings a boatload of souls, changed lives, and restored relationships. I'm convinced that the key to fishing for men is being faithful to cast and cast again.

I'm convinced that the key to fishing for men is being faithful to cast and cast again.

I've preached many times where, when I come down from the pulpit during the invitation, the devil whispers to me, *That was terrible! Nobody's going to get saved after that sorry message.* Then I cast again. And again. Suddenly I see movement from the back of the auditorium . . . .

A high school athlete whose grandmother had prayed for years that he would follow Christ comes down with tears in his eyes.

A couple follows and bends their knees at the altar to recommit their marriage.

A child follows close behind to profess her faith in Christ.

In a valley of dry bones, I watch as the holy breath of God brings life and vibrancy to a church. And I think to myself, *What if I had listened to the enemy and stopped preaching weeks ago? I would have missed it. I would have missed the thrill of seeing God at work!* I have to remind myself and the devil, that God is the One who offers the invitation, and He is the only One who can save.

I was in a revival a few years ago, and the Holy Spirit was so at work. When it came time to give the invitation, the Holy Spirit moved with power and authority. I closed my Bible around eight that evening after preaching my lungs out, wondering if anything I said would make a difference in the lives of these people I quickly grew to love. The Spirit began to move in power. Then on the third verse of the invitation song, stuff happened. It was like wave after wave of the Spirit flowed graciously over the room. People came forward to be saved, to submit everything to God, and to lay everything on the altar. People were healed, marriages got a good dose of hope from the Healer. Time flew as we directed counselors and ministers to pray with those who responded. The boat was brimming! Expectation and elation washed over that auditorium. At 9 p.m., not a single person had left, except for the pastor—but he appeared soon enough in the baptistery. On that one single evening, we saw ten people baptized with a number of other public commitments. Preacher, don't let the devil discourage you! God is at work even after the tenth cast of the net.

The invitation looms over every point and illustration of the message. It's why we preach. We don't preach to infuse a happy mood in the lives of people. We don't preach to make people feel good about who they are or for the admiration of men. We preach for transformation and regeneration. When I preach, I want to be the mouthpiece of God telling a crowd of hungry, helpless people where to find bread.

PRAY FOR THE HARVEST

As I wrote in the first chapter, everything begins with prayer. It begins in Spurgeon's "boiler room."[17] You must be invested in prayer. If you are beginning a season of revival in your church, I hope that you start praying weeks (not days) before the first service. I hope that you have your team every week praying for Sunday. Your prayer room shouldn't simply be a fancy room with comfortable chairs, intricate doilies, and Precious Moments figurines. For a true spiritual

---

17. A term Charles Spurgeon used for the scores of intercessors below the auditorium who prayed throughout the worship services.

awakening, the prayer room must be the foxhole. Don't just lean into an "air war" of preaching. You need boots on the ground, praying and invading enemy territory. Prayer is the real theatre of war. Only then can you truly extend the invitation.

MAKE THE "ASK"

This seems like a no-brainer, but today it needs to be said over and over. In order for people to do something, you have to tell them how to respond. As an old preacher once told me, "Nobody's comin' if they don't know they're invited." Decide from the start what you are asking them to do. If you don't ask, they won't come. And I can tell you that people aren't being asked like they used to be. Preachers often trip over themselves, almost apologizing their way through the invitation. Let me just challenge you: Put your big boy pants on and extend a strong, undeniable, unapologetic invitation.

Remember the story of the lepers at the gates of Syria? They were starving to death, ruminating on the question, *Do we knock on the gates and ask for food, or do we starve to death? They are our enemies, but what do we have to lose? We are probably going to die anyway.* They knock. No answer. And then they realize that there's food, money, and everything they needed to survive the famine inside the walls of the city. They start to enjoy themselves and then they come to their senses. Let's pick up the story in 2 Kings 7:8-9:

> *And when these lepers came to the outskirts of the camp, they went into one tent and ate and drank, and carried from it silver and gold and clothing, and went and hid them; then they came back and entered another tent, and carried some from there also, and went and hid it. Then*

they said to one another, "We are not doing right. This day is a day of good news, and we remain silent."

Through the grace of Jesus, we have everything we need for eternity! If we don't extend the invitation, *we are not doing right!* (Yes, that's me screaming again.) We shouldn't hide the blessings of God. We must make the "ask!"

SO, TELL THEM WHAT YOU WANT THEM TO DO

Again, for those who have been in church since they attended a church meeting nine months before they were born, how you respond to an invitation seems like a presumption. Today it's not. Be sure to challenge people to come down to the front and make their decision public. Invite them to come down during the invitation to pray at the altar. State clearly the decisions they may be called to make. Coming down to the altar to pray should be a natural response, and the more your core members use the altar, the more people will be encouraged to make public decisions. You don't need to make it easy. You just need to make it clear. Let them know clearly the kinds of decisions that God calls people to make:

- To receive the gift of salvation
- To surrender their lives more completely
- To come back to God (rededication)
- To be baptized
- To restore their marriage
- To surrender to preach or to full-time ministry
- To repent of sin
- To ask for public prayer for physical healing

This is an abridged list. I've had people make a public decision to quit smoking, to recommit to sharing the gospel, and even to reconcile with a deacon. The palette is wide when it comes to invitation time. Don't limit it to only two.

LEAVE YOUR INSECURITY AT THE DOOR

I've counseled many discouraged pastors who go through dry seasons in their ministry. They begin to feel worthless because the visible response isn't there. It just ain't happenin'. They look to their right and to their left and it seems like other churches are growing. They question their calling. They go to the evangelism conference and hear stories of mighty victories and wonder what is wrong with them. They preach the Word, and they judge their success on the basis of other's experiences. They suffer from the "not enough" syndrome. They see themselves as not good enough, not smart enough, not popular enough. Their flesh crept into the game.

You can't be hounded by "not enough." You are the one He called. It's not about you. Once you get over yourself, you can stand at the end of the sermon and boldly call people to Jesus.

I want to challenge you with three holy words: *just stop it!* If God wanted good looks and popularity, he would have called Brad Pitt. But last time I checked *People* Magazine, Brad Pitt isn't preaching. *You* are. You can't be hounded by "not enough." You are the one He called. It's not about you. Once you get over yourself, you can stand at the end of the sermon and boldly call people to Jesus. And what if they reject you? Remember the words of Jesus:

> *"He who hears you hears Me, he who rejects you rejects Me, and he who rejects Me rejects Him who sent Me."*
> *(Luke 10:16)*

Like my old high school coach, I believe God is saying to preachers everywhere, "Stop looking at the scoreboard. Look at me! Keep your head in the game." If you're faithful, prayerful, and passionate about the Word, you'll eventually see people come to Jesus. But it won't happen by placating, exaggerating, or commiserating.

EVANGELIZE EVERY TIME YOU PREACH

No service is complete without a clearly articulated presentation of the gospel. If your message is not primarily evangelistic, conclude with prayer and then take a minute to pivot and share the plan of salvation. Why? Because this might be the only chance you get to do that with some people. It's too important to leave out. In fact, I've known men who've gotten saved at pastors' conferences! You just never know who needs to hear the gospel plainly and purposefully.

PRAY BEFORE THE INVITATION

As mentioned previously, I challenge you to pray after the message and before you cast the net. This prayer isn't a tool for transition or a nice way to sneak the musician up on the platform. This should be a passionate prayer spoken not to people but to God. Storm the gates of heaven with your requests.

Ask God to give people the boldness to take the invitation time as a time for miracles and transformation. Beg God to soften the hearts of the congregation. Ask God for big things to happen. Give this time completely to Him. Ask God to tear down the walls of doubt, insecurity, and inhibition. This could be the most important moment in the life of one solitary person. Treat it as such!

HAVE A PLAN

If you are truly expecting people to accept your invitation, you'd better have a plan. Train your people in decision counseling. You've probably seen pastors who didn't have a plan for multiple decisions, and they ended up trying to juggle multiple decisions at one time all by themselves.

If you want a lot of fish, you'd better have a plan to pull them onboard with all hands on deck. If you expect people to come, you're going to need some help. It's not just about filling out cards. Filling out cards is not the reason people come down the aisle of the church. They come because they just had an encounter with the Almighty.

CELEBRATE!

Many times, I've watch people get saved who the entire church has prayed for for many years. It is always exciting to see people rejoice when they see their prayers answered as the lost come down to be saved. When people respond to an invitation, make sure you create a celebration that is comparable to the birth of a baby, because it is just as important and astounding. This isn't an initiation ceremony at the Moose Lodge! This is spiking the ball in the end zone! If you embody the celebration when you announce decisions that were made, your people will too! And a primary side effect of your enthusiasm is that they will want to evangelize so they can celebrate day after day, Sunday after Sunday, invitation after invitation.

So, who wants to fish? I can't wait until I get a chance to go again.

SUMMARY: EXTEND THE INVITATION

- Pray for the harvest
- Make the ask
- Tell them what you want them to do
- Leave your insecurity at the door
- Evangelize every time you preach
- Pray before the invitation
- Have a plan
- Celebrate

JOURNAL THIS

1. Who was the last person you shared the gospel with on a day other than Sunday?

2. Who helps you during the invitation time?

3. What are you praying God will do this year during the
   invitation time?

6

AFTER PREACHING

What happens after you preach is important. I'd like to propose that you do a few things after you've closed the Bible, extended the invitation, and prayed the benediction. As preachers, the message doesn't end after the sermon. Often people will forget what you preached by the time the next Sunday or revival service rolls around. So I hope you won't set it and forget it. Here are seven finishing actions after you've preached.

1. BE PREPARED TO ENGAGE

Many people wouldn't walk the aisle any more than they would walk the plank. It's imperative that we prepare to engage with people when they make comments or ask questions about the message. These times become fertile fields for transformation. Many people want to unpack through dialogue. They need to ask questions, share their experiences and doubts. Be prepared to be as bold in conversation as you were in the pulpit. Challenge them to get closer to God. Plead with them to convert. Implore them to make their decision public. Many times this begins over coffee or on the phone. Be prepared to ask them questions regarding the message you preach. Be conversational and open to their responses. When they make the first move toward you, step boldly in circumstance. This is the most important aspect of the process of post-preaching activity. Remember, after the net has been cast and drawn in, there's still a blue ocean of fish out there.

2. SAY "THANK YOU"

This might seem like a given; however, many preachers feel awkward receiving compliments after the message. What do you say? Do you dismiss the remark with an excuse that it wasn't as good as you had hoped it would be? Should you offer a stumbling, sanctimonious, stained-glass preacher response? Believe me, it's not that complicated. My dad offered me this response: "Son, say, 'Thank you!' And then when you get alone with the Lord, give those 'thank yous' back to Him." Don't apologize for anything. That only draws attention to yourself and away from the real purpose of the message.

3. GET FEEDBACK

Perhaps you have skilled preachers in your church or other preachers who can hear your messages online—don't be shy to ask for feedback. This could be your most valuable tool for improving your message. It takes courage to hear feedback. If it hurts, you might want to test the Spirit and ask why it is so painful. Your ego may be exposed.

Don't be shy to ask for feedback. This could be your most valuable tool for improving your message.

Sometimes you'll discover little distracting things that you were not even aware existed.

One pastor was unaware that he had a tendency to button and unbutton the second button of his coat. He was a dynamic preacher who didn't realize that some of the listeners were spending more time counting how many times he did it than focusing on the words he was saying. Easy fix! I know a pastor who asked for feedback. It was painful to hear his fellow pastor tell him that he used too many illustrations from TV shows and movies. Easy fix! Still another pastor was aided by feedback that his messages were usually extended by his inability to get to the point. Easy fix! Some fixes really are easy, and some are not, but your growth as a preacher should always continue.

I've been preaching for over thirty years, and I know that I still have room for improvement. This makes the craft of preaching so interesting. We can always get better. It's called being a good steward of our gifts.

4. UNDERSCORE THE MESSAGE THROUGHOUT THE WEEK AHEAD

If you are a pastor, you have an opportunity to underscore the message you preach in your emails and newsletters. Find a way to remind your church of the main idea of your message. This will quickly become an extension of your message. If you are on Facebook or Twitter, share a key point of your message as a post or tweet. These little reminders extend the shelf life of your message.

5. ARCHIVE YOUR MESSAGE

Develop a strategy of filing and archiving the messages that you preached—when they were preached and any supporting materials you used such as outlines, illustrations, texts, cross-references, and supporting media. We have a vast array of tools these days. Along with the old faithful disciple of hard-copy filing, we have Google Docs, Dropbox, computer folders, online private blogs, and One Drive—to name a few. The great thing about computer files is that you have search capabilities to discover files, analyze the balance of your biblical text usage, and reaffirm when you used an illustration. Also, many of these tools are cloud based so that if your computer dies, you haven't lost all the work you've done over the years.

Find what works best for you and make it a part of your weekly schedule. It'll only take a couple of minutes, and you'll be so glad you did it.

6. PRAY FOR THE LOST

The Holy Spirit can do amazing things throughout the week with the message you preached on Sunday. The battle continues, and if you pray for it, your message will continue to reverberate in the hearts of the lost.

Sometimes the service ends and you see no response. Don't stop praying for a response after the service ends. The Holy Spirit can do amazing things throughout the week with the message you preached on Sunday. The battle continues, and if you pray for it, your message will continue to reverberate in the hearts of the lost.

7. PRAY FOR RETENTION

Finally, pray for God's Word to sink deeply into the hearts of the listeners. Time and time again, I've had people come to me and say things like this: "In the late 90s, you preached a sermon that changed me." Then they will proceed to share a little of what I preached on and why it meant so much to them at that particular moment in their lives. During those moments I'll often think to myself, *I don't even remember those words coming out of my lips!* But I get excited that God's Word did what it does so well. It grows roots in the hearts of those who have ears to hear.

SUMMARY: AFTER PREACHING

- Be prepared to engage
- Say "thank you"
- Get feedback
- Underscore the message throughout the week
- Archive your messages
- Pray for the lost
- Pray for retention

JOURNAL THIS

1. What causes you the most insecurity after you preach?

2. How do you plan to build your momentum from this week to next week?

3. What's your system for archiving your messages?

AFTERWORD

Over the years, God has revealed that I was born to preach. How about you? Do you have a burning desire to preach the truth of the gospel? My heart breaks when I hear stories from pastors about the battle they face every day.

I've heard the stories of churches and leaders wrestling with the carnage of the opioid crises in their backyard.

I've wept with leaders caught in the grip of pornography.

I've seen Satan tear apart marriages, whisper lies to our children, and wreak havoc in our government.

I've seen the tears of mothers who've seen their kids walk away from their faith and daddies who've seen their sons fall into the grip of addiction.

I've seen the devastation and remorse of abortion.

And I've seen the church, the bride of Christ, arguing over the color of their carpet while the world sinks into the pit of hell.

It's time for churches and pastors to unite. It's time for watchmen on the wall and warriors who are battle tested and ready to take back what the enemy has stolen. It's time to come together as preachers to harvest the fields of our Lord.

When are we, the holy church of Jesus, going to rise up and preach the Word with boldness and authority? When are we going to wake up to the battle? When will the gospel so penetrate souls that we can't help but speak its glorious truth? Can you hear our Savior crying out to the church—*Wake up, O slumbering bride, wake up!*

You can do this! And I am with you—He declares to us today!

He's not looking at the government. He's not looking at the schools. He's looking at the church! And He's looking at you, preacher! It's time to heed His call and *wake up!* And when we do, I have no doubt the enemy will experience the foretaste of his demise.

I want to challenge you to stand, to fight, to *win!*

Pastors: when the forces surround you, and there seems to be nowhere to go but down . . . when you have been challenged, attacked, battered, and thrashed . . . when you have been ridiculed and mocked, accused, subjugated, and hammered . . . you'll be like the house that Jesus built.

The winds will come, and the waves will come crashing down, but you will stand! You will stand because God's people stand on a solid foundation: "On Christ the Solid Rock I stand, all other ground is sinking sand!"[18]

It's time to stand, preacher. We must stand . . . like Moses before Pharaoh;

like Shadrack, Meshack, and Abednego before Nebuchadnezzar; like David before a huge, undefeated, bloodthirsty giant. We will stand—we *must* stand—like Jesus at the flaming portals of hell, demanding the keys!

Undistracted,

Undenied,

Undeterred.

Totally determined, with no thought of retreat.

Burn the ships,

Destroy the bridges.

We are not going back!

You've been called by the One and only God who is all-powerful, all-loving, and all-knowing. Now is the time!

There are victories to be celebrated, sermons to be preached, and a generation to be rescued. There are blessings in the battle.

Let's go win some!

---

18. "On Christ the Solid Rock I Stand," by Edward Mote (1797–1874).

RESOURCES

Preach The Word
Sample Outline
2 Timothy 4:1-5

Introduction: In v. 1, Paul reminds Timothy of the seriousness of his call. He, as well as all believers, will stand before the Lord and give an account for our service to Him.

I.   **Preach the Word (v. 2)**
   a.   The Word of God is living and sharper than a two-edged sword
   b.   The Word of God can and does say far more than we could ever say
   c.   Paul's command was for Timothy to go on the offense:
      i.   **Preach**—*kerusso*—to proclaim or herald
      ii. **The Word**—the content of what He would preach—God's Word—Truth!
      iii. **Ready**—like a soldier ready to go to battle at a moment's notice, always prepared
      iv. **Season**—in season and out of season; when convenient or not (Jeremiah 20:9: "fire shut up in my bones")
   d.   *Specifically*, Timothy was to preach the Word with intent:
      i.   **Reprove**—(mind) correcting false doctrine or ungodly actions with the Word of Truth—this was to convince in the mind—reveal the Truth

      ii. **Rebuke**—(heart) literally, to bring a person under conviction—state the truth in such a manner that the Holy Spirit then brings conviction to the hearer

     iii. **Exhort**—*parakaleo*—come alongside—Paraklete—Comforter, Holy Spirit—we are to encourage those who have been reproved and rebuked

  e. This preaching was to be accomplished with **Perseverance** (long-suffering), **Patience**—don't become exasperated with those you are seeking to reprove, rebuke, and exhort

  f. **Instruction**—must teach from the Word of God: Truth! The Bible is the supreme instruction manual

II. **Expect Opposition (v. 2–4)**

  a. **Time**—seasons—will come—not endure—b/c intolerant

  b. **Sound Doctrine**—literally, "healthy" teaching, that which nourishes

  c. **Desire ear tickling**—someone to overlook their false teaching and sinfulness; someone who will not reprove or rebuke, just encourage **(anyone who holds to Truth is unloving)**

  d. Find teachers that will say what they want to hear—**there are plenty available**

  e. **Will turn away** . . . from truth—**active**—it is intentional that they reject Truth

  f. **Will turn to fables** . . . myths—**passive**—once you have turned from Truth, you are vulnerable for untruth—myths, fables, lies

III. **Endure till the End (v. 5)**

    a. **Be Sober**—not intoxicated, level-headed, under control, steadfast

    b. **Endure hardship**—suffer evil—when you stand firmly on Truth and proclaim it, you will face the onslaught of the enemy and must endure evil

    c. **Evangelist**—office of ministry, speaks of one who is an *evangel*—to herald the Truth, the work of—witness to people

    d. **There are many things that we have to overcome today in doing the work of an evangelist. Many false teachings, universalism, good enough (worthy), works salvation, etc.**

    e. **Fulfill your ministry**—to bring to completion; complete your task!

Look Up
Sample Outline
Psalm 3:1-8

I. **The Attackers (v. 1)**

    a. The number of my attackers is growing

    b. There are more and more against

    c. David, rebellion of Absalom, he was gaining followers

    d. When the adversity comes it seems they are many—they are increasing

II. **The Assault (v. 2)**

    a. They say there is **no help—prolonged cruel or unjust treatment**

    b. Not only is there **opposition** but the **lie that the opposition is perpetrating** is that there is **no help! NOT even in God**

    c. The **strategy** of the enemy is:

        i. You are terribly **outnumbered**, and the adversaries are growing in number

        ii. You are **isolated**—alone

        iii. No one can help you, **not even God**

        iv. He, **God, has forsaken** you

    d. The **battleground is the mind** and the adversaries of David are doing a good job

    e. Your enemy, **the devil,** follows the same pattern; he wants you to believe:

        i. You are terribly **outnumbered**, and your adversaries are growing

        ii. You are all alone—**isolated**

iii. No one can help you, **not even God**

iv. **God has forsaken** you

Selah . . . musical pause: "There, what do you think of that?" This is a pause—time or season!

III. **The Assurance (v. 3–8)**

    a. **But Thou, O Lord—The Devil Is a Liar—But Thou, O Lord!**

    b. You **have not been forsaken!** David explains it for us

    c. **God is my Shield**—He is a buckler on my sides and front and back; He has surrounded me with His shield of protection

    d. **Our God will never leave you unprotected!**

    e. **He is my Glory**—that means that the only glory that comes from the situation will belong to the Deliverer!

    f. **He is the Lifter of my head**—God lifted David's head from defeat but also to see what God was doing! He lifted his head and:

    g. **I cried to the Lord**—He heard

        i. Ever felt like your prayers were not getting through

        ii. Ever felt like God was on vacation or just not listening

        iii. He is always listening—call on Him, cry to Him—He always hears His children

Selah . . . pause of faith: "There, what do you think of that?"

    h. I slept—only the Lord can give you sleep in the midst of the storm

        i. I awoke because the Lord had sustained me

        ii. He will not always take you out of your storm, but He will sustain you in the midst of the storm

  i. I am not afraid

        i. Not of tens of thousands of people that come against me

        ii. Remember—v. 1: "Many are they that rise up against me"

        iii. No matter the number—**no fear** when you are walking with the Lord

  j. I will let the Lord fight for me—arise and save me

        i. Not necessarily a request but more of an expectation

        ii. God has already smitten—to hit, to strike—literally, to strike dead!

        iii. Upon the cheek—insulting, also will knock you out

        iv. Broken their teeth—took their bite away

  k. I will glory in the God of salvation

        i. God is the Deliverer! David recognized Him as the only One who could deliver him from his adversaries

        ii. God is your Deliverer.

Selah . . . pause of peace: "There, what do you think of that?"

CPSIA information can be obtained
at www.ICGtesting.com
Printed in the USA
LVHW032138230323
742467LV00027B/862

9 781613 146149